AMERICAN SETTLEMENTS AND MIGRATIONS:

A Primer for Genealogists and Family Historians

By
Lloyd de Witt Bockstruck
A.B. cum laude, M.S., F.N.G.S., F.T.G.S.

Clearfield Company
Baltimore, Maryland

Printed for Clearfield Company by
Genealogical Publishing Company
Baltimore, Maryland
2017

ISBN 978-0-8063-5831-4

Made in the United States of America

Table of Contents

Chapter One: American Settlements and Migrations

This work covers the colonial and federal periods to the end of the nineteenth century for the British Empire, the United States of America, and for territories acquired by the United States. Tracing an American family from the twenty-first century back to the colonial period is a subject that family historians seek to accomplish. Identifying the founder of the family in the New World and pinpointing his or her origins in the ancestral country have long been goals.

There are three very good works covering the subject: Bernard Bailyn, *The Barbarous Years, The Peopling of British North America: the Conflict of Civilization, 1600-1675* (New York: Alfred A. Knopf, 2012), David Hackett Fischer's *Albion's Seed: Four British Folkways in America; an Ethnic and Ecological Interpretation* (New York: Oxford University Press, 1989), and Terry G. Jordan-Bychkov, *The American Backwoods Frontier: An Ethnic and Ecological Interpretation.* (Baltimore, Md.: John Hopkins University Press, 1989). A thorough knowledge of history and geography is an essential ingredient in tracing an American family. Genealogists well grounded in these fields should be able to identify the three earliest colonies of England in North America. Jamestown was the first in 1607, Bermuda the second in 1612, and Plymouth the third in 1620.

Before Jamestown in 1607 and Plymouth in 1620, Europeans had visited what would be twenty-four of the lower forty-eight states. Contrary to popular perception, America was not an unknown world at the time of European colonization in North America. Even though the English were Protestants seeking to counterbalance the presence of the Spanish and Portuguese who were Roman Catholics, the first Protestant settlement in the New World was Fort Caroline, Florida, New Spain, founded by Huguenots refugees.

The oldest European family in the United States was established by Vicente Solano, who married in St. Augustine, Florida, in New Spain in 1594. Robert Beheathland, who arrived in Virginia in 1607, founded the oldest English family in America, although he had no sons to perpetuate his surname. His two daughters, Mary Beheathland and Dorothy Beheathland, used it as a forename for their offspring. The descendants of Dorothy bestowed it upon males and the descendants of Mary on females. In the Spanish Southwest, Don Pedro Gomez y Chavez settled in New Mexico in 1615. The oldest families at New Netherland were those established by Joris Rapalje and Philippe Truax. Thomas Lewis was the earliest Irish settler in New Amsterdam, where his name became Thomas Ladowycksen. Robert Claflin of Wenham and James Claghorn founded the two oldest Scots families in New England. The Welshmen, Griffith Bowen and Evan Thomas, were the progenitors of the two oldest Welsh families in New England. The earliest Irish were represented by Darby Field in New Hampshire and James Redway in Rehoboth, Massachusetts.

Colonists who obtained citizenship as foreign born, including the English who were born off English soil (including those born at sea), by denizations and naturalizations are covered in Lloyd de Witt Bockstruck's, *Denizations and Naturalizations in the British Colonies in America, 1607-1775.* (Baltimore: Genealogical Publishing Co., 2005).

From the Isle of Man in the north Irish Sea, which was owned by the British, came Capt. Miles Standish who was probably the first Manx to settle in North America. New Jersey and Virginia attracted most of them. John Kaighn came before 1682 and died in New Jersey in 1724. Robert Looney was from Maughold and died in Botetourt County, Virginia in 1769. Many of his descendants use Luna for their surname.

At New Sweden, present day Delaware, Pennsylvania, and New Jersey, the earliest families were founded by Israel Helm, Joran Kyn, and Peter Gunnarsoon. The oldest Finnish family in the colony was established by Henry Hopman. New Netherland was the epitome of ethnic diversity. Hans Hansen Bergen came from Norway. David Tournear from France, Pietro Caesare Alberti from Italy, the Rev. Johannes Theodorus Polhemius from the Rhineland, Dr. Hans Kiersted from Saxony, Christian Barentsen Van Horn from East Friesland, and Evert Jansen Wendel from Hanover became Dutch colonists.

In the English colonies, there was Peter Tallman from Hamburg who settled in Rhode Island; James Freed Torgisen from Scandinavia who settled in New Hampshire. George Heck, a native of Cologne, lived in the colonies of New Netherland, Maryland, and Virginia. Jacob Remey and James Thelabell were from France and settled in Virginia. Nicholas Martiau, a French Huguenot, produced a number of notable descendants including George Washington. Besides Nicholas Martiau being the earliest American progenitor of the nation's first president, he was also the ancestor of another notable descendant, Queen Elizabeth II.

The term "colonist" is one used to encompass those Europeans and Africans who came to North America prior to the independence of the United States from Great Britain. The term "immigrant" connotes someone born outside of the United States who arrived after 1783.

The term "emigrant" designates one who has left his home country. In his new home, he becomes an immigrant.

The period from the planting of the first successful English colony in North America at Jamestowne, Virginia in 1607 to the aftermath of the Civil War in 1865, witnessed the occupation of 407,000,000 acres, and the improvement of another 1,000,000 acres.

While these figures are indeed indicative of the greatest population movement on the globe, the score of years between 1870 and 1890 saw the occupation of another 407,000,000 acres and the cultivation of another 225,000,000 acres.

The study of migrations is inextricably intertwined with family history. By combining a knowledge of history and geography, the family historian can extend the family pedigree across the country. Some members of the family may not have ventured away from the ancestral home. Others went westward but did not continue as far as some of their kinfolk. They may have generated the records further inland which would enable the family historian to bridge an ancestral geographical gap. Finding earlier places of residence could enable one to determine the place of nativity of an ancestor. Following such paths could enable one to locate relatives who remained in the East or dropped off earlier along the migration route, thereby identifying the immigrant or colonist who founded the family in the New World and perhaps the ancestral home in the Old World as well.

On occasion the forenames and surnames borne by one's ancestors may provide the sole clue to extending the pedigree. *In Building an American Pedigree, A Study in Genealogy* (Provo, Utah: Brigham Young University Press, 1974), Dr. Norman Edgar Wright demonstrated how a surname might be identified by ethnic group and locality of origin where the surname arose. For example, Zeigenfuz or Zeigenfoot was an occupational surname used by a particular family in a small eastern German village. Members of one family in the village were clockmakers, and the second hand on the clock was a swinging foot or Zeigenfuz. Their occupation became their surname.

Settlers may or may not have created the records in which they appeared. The clerks who did so may have had different accents; they may have been illiterate; or they may have been of different nationalities. The New England family of Hobart also appeared as Hubbard. The Andrews family could have become Andros, Andress, and Indress. The Briggs family may have been Bridges. Seymour and Elmore could have been males who appeared in the records at Charles C. Moore and John L. Moore. The Virginia family of Burroughs eventually became Burrus, Royal became Rial, and some of the Stockton family appeared as Stogden. British subjects who were in French or Spanish territory also shed their surnames for ones more suitable. The Irish surname of O'Brien became Obregon in New Spain and Littlefield became Litrefils in New France.

Forenames are not so likely to have been modified, and they can be clues to a family's background. Evan, Rhys, and Owen are Welsh. Ian, Neil, Stewart, Kenneth, Donald, and Douglas are borne by Scottish Highlanders. Duncan, Colin, Gavin, Nicol, Alexander, Jean, Agnes, Jane, and Isabella are Scottish. Ulrich, Benedict, and Vincent are not only German but common for Germans from Switzerland. Teunis is Dutch. Patrick was common throughout the Emerald Isle, and was widespread among both the Roman Catholic Irish and the Presbyterian Ulster-Scots.

The prefix "O" is Gaelic for grandson of. Members of the Austin family had their surname spelled Osteen, so there is more than one origin of the prefix. The prefix "von" is German. "Van" is most commonly Dutch, but it does appear in German. In the Van Swearingen family it actually became a forename and disappeared as a prefix. Van is also the diminutive of the forename Sylvanus.

Non-British families may have altered their surnames to their English counterparts. The German Klein family adopted the spelling of its surname as Cline. Others became Little, Short, and Small. For more examples see Lloyd deWitt Bockstruck's *The Name Is the Game*: *Onomatology and the Genealogist* (Baltimore: Clearfield, 2004).

There are several principles of migration. Firstly, one must understand the local history of one's ancestral homes. If one were to take a map of the adjacent 48 states in the nation in 1950 and identify the state which had the greatest percentage of residents who were of British descent, it would not necessarily be obvious. It was not Virginia or Massachusetts. It was the trans-Mississippi state of Utah. The state was settled by members of the Church of Jesus Christ of latter-Day Saints commonly referred to as the Mormons. This religious group was established in western upstate New York by Joseph Smith, a native of Vermont. The Mormons were descended from New England Puritan stock. Hundreds of Mormons migrated westward to Kirtland, Ohio. Ten thousand Mormons then removed to Missouri only to re-cross the Mississippi River to settle at Nauvoo, Illinois, before making their final trek to Utah. Their first missionary efforts abroad were in the British Isles, and these converts joined them in Utah.

Secondly, migrations are also tied to similar climatic belts. Colonists and immigrants sought out lands that were capable of growing the crops with which they were familiar. It is important to be aware of geography. For example, the state of Mississippi is farther south than any part of Europe. All of the British Isles are farther north on the globe than Maine or any other state in the lower forty-eight.

The colonial governments sought to capitalize on their main asset–land. Warfare with other New World powers led to the adoption of bounty and donation land policies that enabled those without the financial means to acquire realty. Governments at all levels–municipal, colony, and imperial–followed such policies. Some governments offered land at enlistment or retroactively after the conflict. Bounty land was offered as an inducement to enlist and remain in the service. Donation land grants were awarded after the following conflicts:

1646	Pequot War
1675-1676	King Phillips' War
1689-1693	King William's War
1702-1713	Queen Anne's War
1740-1748	War of Jenkins's Ear or King George's War 1745-1748 or War of Austrian Succession 1740-1748
1754-1763	French and Indian War or the Seven Years War
1763-1764	Pontiac's War

Lloyd de Witt Bockstruck's *Bounty and Donation Land Grants in British Colonial America* (Baltimore: Genealogical Publishing Co., 2007) covers these conflicts.

In the southern colonies, diseases such as malaria, yellow fever, dysentery, typhoid fever, and enteritis were responsible for the high death rate. Colonists in Massachusetts survived these scourges because of the colder seasons that killed off the bacteria. The same cold weather in New England increased the risk of pulmonary infections for African slaves and accounts for their smaller numbers there.

Thirdly, migration rests upon forces that draw immigrants to a new home. It may also apply to those forces that drove them away from their home. In some instances both aspects may apply.

If one were to divide the trans-montane states into three layers with the upper tier consisting of Ohio, Indiana, and Illinois; the middle tier consisting of Tennessee, Kentucky, and Missouri; and the lower tier consisting of Georgia, Alabama, Mississippi, Louisiana, and Texas, which tier would have the most residents who were natives of Virginia in 1850? It would be the upper tier of the Old Northwest where more than a hundred and fifty-two thousand Virginians resided. They settled in the areas accessible to them and sought out a terrain and soils with which they were familiar.

Settlers exist in groups or clusters, so if one cannot trace the path of a given ancestor, studying his associates and neighbors may yield the name of the ancestral home. Sometimes the group was composed of family relatives if not by consanguinity then by affinity. An ancestor may have attached himself to his wife's kinfolk and her maiden name was unknown, but by studying the neighbors, her maiden identity might be discovered. Other groups may have been bound by religion or ethnicity.

Colonial migrations are in contrast with those after independence. During the colonial period, individuals and groups moved from the southern colonies to the northern colonies, and those in the northern colonies moved to the southern colonies. Until the 1750s, colonists utilized sailing ships as the primary mode of transportation between colonies. They did not move from the East to the West until after the French and Indian War, when the Braddock and Forbes roads were built to enable the military forces to go into the interior to challenge the French in the Ohio River Valley. Roads were necessary to move heavy military equipment, such as canons, and materiel to the war front.

Peter Brown was a passenger aboard the *Mayflower* in 1620. His great-grandson, Peter Raymond, lived in Middleboro, Massachusetts, and moved his family south to Newark, Essex County, New Jersey, where he died in 1760. His daughter, Mercy Raymond, married Jonas Bedford. By 1761 they were in Cumberland County, Pennsylvania, where they bought 600 acres on the Juniata River.

During the French and Indian War, they moved south to the Catawba River valley in Tryon County, North Carolina, where Jonas Bedford died in 1820.

Another example of a north to south migration involved Isaac Allerton, who was a signatory to the Mayflower Compact. He left Plymouth Colony and removed to Maine where he established a trading post. In 1643 he moved to New Amsterdam. He eventually migrated to New London, Connecticut, where he died in 1659. His son, Isaac Allerton, Jr., migrated to Virginia where his daughter, Sarah Allerton, married Hancock Lee. They were the parents of Richard Lee among whose descendants was President Zachary Taylor.

George Hack, a native of Cologne, Germany, studied medicine and became a physician. He came to New Amsterdam in the 1640s and became a partner of Augustine Herman, a native of Prague. George Hack's wife, Ann Verleth, was a sister-in-law of Herman. Hack became involved in the tobacco trade and moved to Northampton County, Virginia, on the Eastern Shore where he died in 1665.

Jost Hite left Europe in 1709 from the port of Rotterdam and settled in Kingston, New York in 1710. In 1716, he moved to Germantown, Pennsylvania. The Indian menace prompted him to take his family to the area around Winchester, Virginia, in the Shenandoah Valley.

American families migrating westward recorded their daily travel distances in miles. Since there were not signposts showing the mileage from one settlement to another, one might wonder how they knew how far they had traveled on any given day. Benjamin Franklin used an odometer to calculate the mileage. As the Postmaster General, he collected postage based on mileage. The device was in use as early as the 1670s.

With the middle colonies being populated by English Quakers in New Jersey and Pennsylvania, the Germans in Maryland and Pennsylvania, and the Scots in Delaware and Pennsylvania, the Quaker State created the new frontier County of Lancaster in the West in order to accommodate the growing number of colonists. In addition to the increasing population, soil depletion due to the cultivation of tobacco in neighboring Delaware, Maryland, and Virginia, and the accompanying waning economic prosperity on the Eastern Shore put pressure on the settlers in these colonies to resettle in lower Pennsylvania until they reached the natural barrier of the Susquehannah River. It was a very broad watercourse and was fordable at only two points in Lancaster County. In the northern part it was Harris's Ferry where the Scots-Irish resided. The other ford was Wright's Ferry thirty miles farther south. The later lay within the area in dispute with the Penn and Calvert families. Beyond the Susquehannah River, the Appalachian mountains were also a natural barrier and blocked westward expansion.

International relations also played a significant part in colonial expansion in the middle colonies. In 1739 Robert Jenkins lost his ear to the Spanish off the coast of Florida in the struggle of empires over the colony of Georgia and a contest of commercial rivalry. France joined the side of the Roman Catholic Spanish. The whole affair mushroomed into King George's War. The war marked the first time that authorities in England referred to the colonists collectively as Americans. The royal governors of Virginia, Maryland, and Pennsylvania, met at Lancaster, Pennsylvania, with representatives of the Six Nations. The Indians agreed to withdraw from the Atlantic coastal plain, leaving the area open to the English. The treaty of 1744 effectively opened the Great Warrior Path and led to its transformation into the Philadelphia Wagon Road.

A war with France jeopardized all of New England and New York, which abutted the French in Quebec and in the Ohio River Valley. The settlers in Pennsylvania and New Jersey were prompted to leave the area. Great Britain issued a proclamation to the governors of Massachusetts, Connecticut, Rhode Island, New Hampshire, New York, New Jersey, Pennsylvania, Maryland, and Virginia, to raise troops to confront the enemy. The Carolinas and Georgia did not have sufficient colonists to be called upon for military service and were exempt. Accordingly, the pacifistic Quakers and pietistic Germans in the middle colonies were motivated to relocate in the Piedmont of North Carolina in 1747 where they did not have to violate their conscience.

Another significant factor in the southward migration was economic. It involved the price of land. There was already a scarcity of good land in Pennsylvania, and the price had been escalating. In 1710, it cost £2 to purchase two hundred acres with an annual quit rent of 1 shilling in Pennsylvania. By 1713, the price was £10 with a quit rent of 1 shilling. By 1732, the price for the same acreage was £15 with a quit rent of 4 shillings and 2 pence. In North Carolina by contrast the same 200-acre tract could be had for 5 shillings. All of these factors had a decided impact on the settlement of the Piedmont of the Carolinas. The colonists were pushed out of their homes by various forces and drawn to new homes for other reasons.

Colonists from Trenton, New Jersey, crossed over into Pennsylvania and traveled westward to Lancaster and York. They crossed the Potomac River and descended to Winchester, Virginia, and Staunton, Virginia, to Big Lick (Roanoke). This was the Great Valley Route.

Others traveled on the Upper Road from Philadelphia to Wilmington, Delaware, and continued to Baltimore, Maryland, and Annapolis, Maryland. The road continued to Amelia Courthouse in Amelia County, Virginia, and then to Hillsboro, Orange County, North Carolina to Salisbury, Rowan County, North Carolina, and Charlotte, Mecklenburg County, North Carolina.

The Fall Line Road left Philadelphia and went through Wilmington, Delaware, to Baltimore and Annapolis, Maryland. It continued to Fredericksburg and Petersburg, Virginia. It crossed into North Carolina at Warrenton. It continued to Cheraw, South Carolina, and terminated at Augusta, Georgia.

Clues as to the origins of those involved in migrations may be geographical. The decision to join the westward movement was a momentous one because most individuals realized that they would not be able to return to their former homes. This nostalgia prompted them to remember whence they had come in their choices of place names.

In New England and elsewhere colonists named their new settlements after their ancestral villages in their mother country. The Hobart family was from Hingham, England, and were original settlers of Hingham, Massachusetts. By 1675 Puritan settlers had named numerous towns after their home villages in England. These included Andover, Barnstaple, Billerica, Boston, Boxford, Braintree, Bridgewater, Cambridge, Chelmsford, Dartmouth, Dedham, Derby, Dover, Dorchester, Exeter, Falmouth, Framingham, Gloucester, Greenwich, Groton, Guilford, Hadley, Haverhill, Hull, Ipswich, Lancaster, Lynn, Malden, Manchester, Marlborough, Medford, Newbury, Newton, Northampton, Norwich, Plymouth, Portsmouth, Reading, Rowley, Salisbury, Southampton, Springfield, Stamford, Stratford, Sudbury, Taunton, Topsfield, Truro, Wallingford, Warwick, Wells, Weymouth, Windsor, Woburn, Wrentham, Yarmouth, and York.

The colony of Maryland was unique in requiring each patentee to name his or her tract of land. John White took up three tracts of land in his lifetime. One he named Buckinghamshire, which is a County in England. Another tract he named Newport Pagnell. That is the name of a parish in

Buckinghamshire. He bestowed the name of Caldecott on the third tract. In a history of the parish is a photograph of one of the oldest structures in the parish, and it was called Caldecott, which was the home of a White family. By focusing on the geographical nomenclature left by John White, a descendant was able to ascertain his ancestral origins. When John Welch secured a tract of land in East Bethlehem Township, Washington County, Pennsylvania, in 1785, he left a clue to his origins in naming the tract "Enniskillen" for his former home in Ireland.

At the mouth of the Neuse river in North Carolina is the city of New Bern. The people who settled the area were from Bern, Switzerland. The river flowing through that city is the Neuse, so these place names provide the best clues for the origins of the first settlers of the area. The original name of the settlement was Neuse Berne. Unfamiliar with German, the English rendered the first word as New.

The counties of York, Lancaster, and Chester in the upcountry of South Carolina were named for their counterparts in Pennsylvania from which the settlers of the Carolina Piedmont hailed. Orange County, Indiana was named for Orange County, North Carolina, from which some of the early settlers came. Norwalk, Ohio, is another example of a place name in the Mid-West named for a place in the East--Norwalk, Connecticut, some of whose residents moved to the Buckeye State. The importance of toponyms should not be overlooked.

The westward movement began in the countries on the eastern boundary of the Atlantic Ocean of Europe and Africa. There were forces in Europe and Africa that pushed them out of the Old World just as there were forces that pulled them to the New World. The urge to relocate could have been for better economic opportunity. Cheaper and better lands were also major forces in migrations. Political and military forces were also at work. Depletion of the soils and overpopulation also affected migrations as did the discovery of the precious metals of gold and silver.

The first gold rush was in 1799 on the farm of John Reed in Cabarrus County, North Carolina. He was a former Hessian soldier; his name was originally Johannes Reith. The next was in Dahlonega, Georgia, in 1828. The California Gold Rush in 1849 was the first migration in the nation in which participants did not adhere to any patterns of migrations. It was a race among individuals to reach the gold fields by any means of transport or route they could. Prospectors abandoned family and friends and headed West. The last gold rushes were in Alaska at Juneau in 1880, Nome in 1898, and Fairbanks in 1902. The California and Alaska rushes also attracted immigrants.

Wild animals had had centuries to trample paths which the American Indians followed in quest of furs and food. The settlers in turn took advantage of these long established trails.

A topographical map of the United States offers the best perspective for understanding migrations. Geography dictated the lives of the settlers and their places of settlement. Columbus and others reached North America by sailing along the west coast of Europe past Spain and Portugal, Gibraltar, the Canary Islands, and northwest Africa, until they reached the currents that which would carry them across the Atlantic ocean. Sea captains knew to veer off into the Atlantic when their butter began to melt.

The North American continent has a coastal plain on the Atlantic seaboard known as the Tidewater. Its inland reach ranges from 50 to 150 miles. It takes its name from the fact that the inland water levels in the rivers that laced it were affected by the tide. The Tidewater was the more recent extension of the continental shelf with the buildup of rich top soil in thin layers. From Maine to Georgia, the tidewater was drained by a number of large rivers namely the Kennebec, Merrimac,

Connecticut, Hudson, Delaware, Susquehanna, Potomac, James, Roanoke, Cape Fear, Pee Dee, Santee, Ashley-Cooper, and Savannah River valleys. These rivers emptied into the Atlantic ocean, and the soils along the river banks were ideal for agriculture. The river bottoms were highly prized. They received heavy rainfall, had warm climates, lacked underbrush to clear out, and teemed with wildlife for food. In the southern colonies water borne diseases made the tidewater unhealthy. The colonists were amazed at the excessive fertility of the soil but failed to understand why the wheat they sowed grew to an average height of seven feet but never headed out. They had to learn from the Indians to plant several seasons of corn in order to drain off the nutrients of the rich soil.

The Blue Ridge Mountain chain had four natural points of egress cut by rivers. They were the Delaware, Susquehannah, Potomac, and the James. Another seventy miles farther west were the Alleghenies, which were 3,000 to 4,000 feet tall and a greater obstacle to westward migration.

In the southern colonies the cash crop became tobacco and later rice, indigo, and cotton. The Tidewater river valleys made possible the riparian penetration of North America.

If the Atlantic coast could have been exchanged with the Pacific coast, European colonization would have been delayed for decades. The lack of natural harbors, the absence of large navigable rivers penetrating the interior, a very narrow tidewater, coastal mountain ranges blocking inland settlement, the even higher Rocky Mountains farther inland, and a semiarid wasteland of inland plateaus, and deserts would have been impossible for colonists to have overcome.

There were very few natural harbors on the west coast of North America as opposed to those on the east coast. At the lower end was San Diego Bay. Farther north, Monterey Bay was a shelter-less and shallow bay. San Francisco Bay was larger than anything in Europe. Los Angeles, Santa Barbara, Portland, and Seattle, had harbors capable of accommodating ocean-going vessels.

On the North American continent, the French took possession of the St. Lawrence and Mississippi River valleys. The Spanish took Florida and the New Southwest. The British controlled the Atlantic seaboard. The Dutch in New Netherland and the Swedes at New Sweden were tiny enclaves surrounded by the British.

The English were motivated by various factors to come to the New World. The Anglicans, as well as the Pilgrims and Puritans, sought to bring salvation to the people of America. Those who settled in New England feared that the Spanish would seize Jamestowne. If the Protestants did not act, North America would become Roman Catholic. The international situation caused the Pilgrims to seek permission for their own colony. Many English believed that they could reach the Pacific from Virginia by portage across the Appalachians.

Between 1607 and 1880 there were 650,000 people who came to the United States, which was less than one person a day. Between 1820 and 1880, 10,000,000 immigrants arrived, which was an average of 400 per day. Between 1880 and 1920, some 25,000,000 immigrants arrived at a rate of 2,000 per day. The sheer numbers help to forecast how much difficulty might be expected in extending a family's pedigree back to the founder of the family and then to an ancestral home in the Old World.

During the colonial era, the period 1607 to 1680 was dominated by the planting of Jamestowne by the Virginia Company of London and by the Puritans to Massachusetts. The era 1640 to 1675 was marked primarily by the flight of the Royalist elite from England to the colonies on the Chesapeake and arrival of indentured servants for the labor force in the Middle Colonies and in the Carribean.

Between 1675 and 1725 the colonists tended to be from the Midlands and Wales and came to the Delaware river valley. The fourth and last period of colonial immigration extended from 1718 to 1775, when most of the colonists left from the borders of North Britain and Ireland for the Appalachian back country.

The ethnic composition was different in each era. From 1607 to 1700 the English, Welsh, Africans, and Huguenots were the main groups arriving. From 1700 to 1775 the English, Welsh, and Africans continued to be significant. They were joined by the Scots-Irish and the Germans. The Revolutionary War brought an end to new arrivals, although German auxiliary troops did constitute a little known group who remained behind. Out of thirty thousand German combatants from the states of Hesse-Cassel, Braunschweig, Hesse-Hanau, Ansbach-Bayreuth, Waldeck, and Anhalt Zerbst, at least five thousand remained in North America. Since the German soldiers were obtained by treaties between sovereign nations, their troops were not mercenaries even though Americans resorted to the use of the term to win support for the war. A mercenary is a private individual hired to be a soldier. King George III was also the Elector of Hanover and a few of his German subjects did enroll for duty in North America. The German auxiliary troops who remained in America settled among other German communities where they were indistinguishable from other colonial Germans.

Between 1820 and 1870 the immigrants from Northwest Europe and the British Isles included the Irish seeking to escape suffering from the Potato Famine, The Germans and the Dutch composed the main infusion of foreign immigration. Between 1870 and 1920 eastern and southern Europe and Scandinavia predominated. These more recent arrivals gravitated to the industrial centers in the north and northeast. It was the greatest period of immigration in the nation's history. From 1920 to 2012, the numbers have been fewer but the variety greater. Asia and Latin America have provided the bulk of the immigrants.

Approximately 540,000 colonists left England between 1630 and 1700, but only 380,000 of that number came to the New World. Of the 69,000 who left in the 1630s, only 21,000 came to New England. By 1700, 39,000 Englishmen had come to New England while 116,000 had come to the Chesapeake Bay and the Southern mainland colonies. By contrast the English colonies in the Caribbean had received 225,000 by the close of the seventeenth century.

In England's last colony, Georgia, the land patents issued between 1754 and 1759 identified Samuel New and his son, James, from Nevis; Andrew Low, Francis Blake, and Heriot Crooke from St. Christopher; Robert Baillie from Jamaica; Adriaan Van Beverhoudt and his three sons from St. Croix; John Hamm and Clement Martin from St. Christopher; William Lee from Barbados; John Jagger, Thomas Bates, and Lemuel Smith from the Bay of Honduras; and Thomas Magee and Peter Yales from Bermuda.

The West Indies and Barbados were England's most prosperous colonies in the seventeenth century. The islands produced sugar cane, tobacco, dye stuff, ginger, and cocoa. The English used indentured servants and transported felons in producing the cash crop of sugar cane. The high death rate and the expiration of their contracts caused the English to turn to slave labor from Africa. They were more accustomed to a tropical climate, and their servitude was for life. Howard Dodson and Sylviane A. Diour's *In Motion: The African-American Migration Experience* (Washington, D.C.: National Geographic, 2014) has some colonial data but primarily treats the twetieth century.

The British colonies in the West Indies were Bermuda in 1612, St. Christopher in 1623, Barbados in 1627, Nevis in 1628, Montserrat in 1632, Antigua in 1632, Anguilla in 1650, Jamaica in 1655, and Tortola in 1672. Between 1640 and 1660 two-thirds of the English immigrants to North America came to the West Indies colonies. By 1650 they had 44,000 settlers when the Chesapeake had only 12,000 and New England 23,000, mostly were primarily indentured servants and criminals.

It is traditionally believed that English or British citizenship did not extend beyond those of European birth or descent; however, there are plenty of examples of American Indians and African Blacks being naturalized in the colonial era. Abemlich, an Indian, was naturalized in Connecticut in 1695 is such an example.

Members of the Society of Friends, more popularly known as Quakers, visited the British Empire and traveled from Great Britain to the colonies, as told in Joseph Besse's *Sufferings of Early Quakers, America–New England & Maryland, West Indies–Antigua, Barbados, Jamaica, and Nevis, Bermuda.* (London: Luke Hinde, 1753). The second volume covers the islands of Barbados, Nevis, Bermuda, Antigua, and Jamaica and contains the names of those persecuted for their faith.

In 1673 King Charles suggested that communications be established among his colonies. The result was a riding trail which, when completed, ran from Boston, Massachusetts to Charleston, South Carolina. Initially it was a mail route, but it expanded to accommodate trade and passengers. The lack of bridges and the absence of pavement reduced activity greatly in the rainy seasons. The King's Highway ran from Boston, Massachusetts; New Haven, Connecticut; Greenwich, Connecticut; Rye, New York; Kingsbridge, New York; New York City, New York;
Newark, New Jersey; Elizabeth, New Jersey; Rahway, New Jersey; Perth Amboy, New Jersey; New Brunswick, New Jersey; Princeton, New Jersey; Trenton, New Jersey; Bordentown, New Jersey; Burlington, New Jersey; Philadelphia, Pennsylvania; Chester, Pennsylvania; Wilmington, Delaware; New Castle, Delaware; Annapolis, Maryland; Alexandria, Virginia; Fredericksburg, Virginia; King William, Virginia; New Kent, Virginia; Williamsburg, Virginia; Yorktown, Virginia; Hampton, Virginia; Norfolk, Virginia; Suffolk, Virginia; Edenton, North Carolina; New Bern, North Carolina; Wilmington, North Carolina; Georgetown, North Carolina; and Charleston, South Carolina. It was eventually 3,000 miles long.

Between the end of the Seven Years' War in 1763 and the Revolutionary War in 1775, more than 55,000 Protestant Irish, 40,000 Scots, more than 33,000 English, 12,000 Germans and Swiss, and 84,500 Africans settled south of New England.

Many colonists seemingly disappear from the records of their home locality in America. In some cases it should be considered that their disappearance was due to the fact that they had returned to their place of nativity. Stephen Tracy is such an example. He was born in Great Yarmouth, England, and came to Plymouth Colony in 1623 on the *Anne*. He returned to England between 1643 and 1652 where he died testate in 1654.

Chapter Two: New England

Directories of colonists who settled New England include Robert Charles Anderson's *The Great Migration Begins: Immigrants to New England, 1620-1633 and 1634-1635* (Boston: New England Historic Genealogical Society, 2011) and *The Winthrop Fleet: Massachusetts Bay Company Immigrants to New England, 1629-1630* (Boston: New England Historic Genealogical Society, 2012) and Alicia Crane Williams, *Early New England Families 1641-1700* (Boston: New England Historic Genealogical Society, 2015). Yankees captured by the French and their Indian allies and taken to Canada are treated in Emma L. Coleman's *New England Captives Carried to Canada between 1677 and 1760 during the French and Indian Wars* (Portland, Maine, Southwest Press, 1925).

New England migrations are treated in Stewart H. Holbrook, *The Yankee Exodus, An Account of Migration from New England.* (Seattle, Washington: University of Washington Press, 1968). Lois K. M. Rosenberry's *The Expansion of New England Settlements and Institutions to the Mississippi River, 1620-1865* (New York: Russell & Russell, 1962) complements Holbrook. Jewish settlers are treated in Leon Huhner, *The Jews of New England [Other than Rhode Island] prior to 1800* (West Cornwell: Cornwell Press, 1973). The series, *Mayflower Families Through Five Generations: Descendants of Pilgrims Who Landed at Plymouth, Mass., December 1620* (Plymouth, Massachusetts General Society of Mayflower Descendants, 1975 ff.) is without equal.

Massachusetts

The Pilgrims were Separatists from England who had sojourned in the Netherlands a few years before setting sail from England for Virginia. Their vessel, the *Mayflower,* landed in November 1620 at Providencetown on Cape Cod. Within a month they had decided to transplant themselves across the bay at a place they called New Plymouth. Robert Charles Anderson covered Plymouth Colony in *The Pilgrim Migration: Immigrants to Plymouth Colony, 1620-1633* (Boston: New England Historic Genealogical Society, 2004). There were 149 passengers aboard, of whom only forty were Separatists. Within the next two decades the colony had expanded with settlements in Scituate in 1633, Hingham 1635, Bridgewater in 1636, Duxbury in 1637, Sandwich and Barnstable in 1638, and Taunton and Yarmouth in 1639. Massachusetts lacked navigable rivers into the interior so the expansion of settlement clung to the coast. The shoals off Cape Cod made it necessary for inter-coastal movement and reliance on overland routes.

The Pilgrims were aware that the word "Sinai" meant brambles. They believed that the forests of Cape Cod confined and persecuted the church as in Pharoah's Egypt. To them the *Mayflower* was the true church. It carried the fear of God as its ballast. Its sails represented faith and its masts the cross. The wind was the Holy Spirit carrying them to the New World. England was the land of Egypt, and the Atlantic Ocean was the Red Sea. The voyage corresponded to Paul's journey to Rome.

The success of Plymouth Colony was due to the harvest of beaver pelts. At least one Greek writer had reported that the Magi wore beaver hats so there was a spiritual association as well. By the 1630s the Pilgrims were shipping more than two thousand pelts annually back home to England. The beaver trade insured that the Massachusetts Bay Colony would succeed. Samuel Pepys in his diary recorded that he paid £4.5 for a beaver hat. That amounted to three months of wages. Hat makers used mercury to separate the beaver fur from the pelt. Such a practice led to a high incidence of mental illness among those who practiced the trade and gave rise to the expression "mad as a hatter."

Massachusetts Bay Colony was settled by Puritan adherents of the Church of England in 1630. John Winthrop led them. Seventeen vessels made the voyage. Out of the one hundred and ninety-eight vessels which brought the Puritans to North America, only one ship was lost at sea. It was the *Gabriel* lost near Pemaquid, Maine, in 1635. The Great Migration was underway. Twenty-one thousand colonists swelled their numbers. Within the first year the towns of Boston, Medford, Salem, and Watertown were established. Concord, Ipswich, Marblehead, Newbury, and Weymouth were settled within the next five years. The hundreds of families of colonists came directly from England. Within the first decade some twenty-four thousand five hundred more Puritans driven overseas by conditions at home arrived. Some fifteen hundred Puritans settled in Maine and New Hampshire; fourteen thousand in Massachusetts; three hundred in Rhode Island; and two thousand in Connecticut.

Massachusetts was a colony of families. There were one hundred fifty males for every hundred females, in contrast to Virginia where there were four males for every female. By contrast in New Spain there were ten males for every female, and in Brazil there were one hundred males for every female.

Massachusetts was just one of the many places for the English to go. Twenty thousand moved to Ireland, and a similar number went to St. Kitts, Barbados, Old Providence, and Nevis.

The Puritans did without a legislature or general court until forced to form them in 1634. The delegates were from the individual towns. Only freemen could vote or hold political office. In order to be eligible for freeman status, one had to be a member of the church. In order to be a church member, one had to be approved by the clergy. This scheme allowed the Puritans their monopoly of power. Initially, Massachusetts decreed that its the militia members must first be members of the church.

The Puritan migration to Massachusetts came to a halt during the English Civil War, 1642 to 1651, as Puritans returned to England to serve.

Massachusetts provided the planting of town sites by making grants to both individuals and to groups. Ministers, military veterans, school masters, and new towns on the frontier made possible the expansion. It was necessary for several families to petition for a settlement. The leaders made certain that only the orthodox would be approved. Usually the new towns were six mile square but topography and neighboring towns had to be taken into consideration. New towns had to be near established towns for military defense purposes. The town fathers became the proprietors. They could sell the unclaimed land within their borders, they could give it away, and they could devise it to their heirs. The proprietors divided the plot, built the church in the center, located a minister, and recruited the requisite numbers of newcomers. They had two to three years to do so. All of the homes surrounded the church in the town. The livestock could be driven into the village and the apertures closed so that beasts of prey could not kill their sheep and other livestock. Each land owner had several detached pieces of property. He would have a house lot, a barn lot, a garden plot, an orchard, pasture, hay yard, and strips of upland fields. Such an arrangement allowed everyone to enjoy a share of the most desirable portions. The amount of land allocated to each head of household was based on his wealth. Colonists were not isolated rural settlers, as they were in the Chesapeake.

Massachusetts had a population that doubled every generation for two centuries. By 1700 the

Yankee population was a hundred thousand. Most of those who came in the Great Migration came in families.

Family size in New England was much larger than in the southern colonies. The winters and nights were longer, so that married couples spent more time in bed together. The muggy, hot weather of the tidewater south discouraged such intimacy. The colder climate in New England also reduced the rate of infant mortality and illness by combating the bacteria. There were fewer children per capita in seventeenth century Virginia. In Plymouth Colony, Pilgrim John Howland at his death left a widow, ten children, and eighty-eight grandchildren. In contrast, in tidewater Virginia, more than three-quarters of the children were in households where one or both of their parents died young. Households in the southern colonies were often composed of orphans, half-siblings, and step-siblings.

It is important to point out that Virginia received eighteen thousand Puritans concurrently with New England. Maryland attracted fifteen hundred Puritans and Bermuda three thousand. As impressive as these figures are, the colony that received the most settlers in the great Puritan migration was Barbados where eighteen thousand six hundred Puritans settled. Massachusetts received fourteen thousand.

Each of the West Indian islands of New Providence, Old Providence, St. Croix, St. Kitts, Barbuda, Antigua, Montserrat, and Santa Lucia received fewer than five hundred each.

In 1636 Indians murdered the Boston renegade, John Oldham. The Pequots boasted that they could defeat any enemy by witchcraft. Massachusetts sent out Capt. John Endicott with ninety soldiers against the Indians to demand the murderers. The soldiers destroyed the villages and crops of the Pequots. The Indians retaliated and slew every Englishman they could find. War was declared 1 May 1637. The Mohegans and Narragansetts remained passive and did not join with the Pequots. Capt. John Mason led a force of a hundred eighty men from Connecticut. He caught the Pequots by surprise and put five hundred of them to death. Mason pursued the survivors, and they were caught in the swamp fight at Fairfield. The war led to the founding of the Ancient and Honorable Artillery Company in Boston to train officers in the military forces as related in Oliver Ayer Roberts, *History of the Military Company of Massachusetts, Now Called the Ancient and Honorable Artillery Company of Massachusetts, 1637-1888* (Boston: A. Mudge and Son, 4 vols., 1895-1901).

New Englanders clung to the Tidewater. Intercommunication among the coastal settlements was easy. The forests were clogged with thick underbrush, so that the English could not penetrate the interior. In fact, the foliage was so thick that sunlight never fell on the ground. As the English peered into the interior, they sometimes saw American Indians with painted faces. From their theological perspective the Kingdom of Darkness was Satan's domain and the faces peering at them were the imps of Hell. In addition to the Indian threat, New Englanders avoided the interior because of the presence of the French in the St. Lawrence Valley. The low mountains were also a barrier, but none of these reasons accounts for the migration along the coast instead of into the interior. It was because they lacked expertise in forest colonization. They had come out of towns and villages in rural England.

New England's land-locked harbors and bays fostered the seafaring trade. The New Englanders preferred a diet of mutton, so they were dependent on raising sheep, and shied away from forests where the natural enemies of their sheep, wolves, lurked.

England was plunged into civil war in 1640. The cavaliers were the defenders of the crown. The term cavalier derived from the Spanish "caballero" which was a corruption of the term used for a Spanish trooper given to torturing Protestants. The war brought an abrupt end to the migration of Puritans to the New World. Hundreds of Puritans from Massachusetts and Connecticut reversed the flow and returned to England to join the rebellion. Seventy percent of the first graduating class of Harvard College did so. During the English civil war following Oliver Cromwell's victory over the Scots at the battle of Dunbar in 1650, a consignment of Scottish prisoners sailed from London to Boston on November 11 aboard the *Unity*. They were sold for £30 each and indentured for seven years. Sixty-two were purchased for working at the ironworks at Lynn. The rest were dispersed to other parts of Massachusetts, Maine, and New Hampshire.

Following the restoration in 1660, several English Puritans and Parliamentarians fled to New Haven, Connecticut. They included John Dixwell, William Goffe, and Edmund Whalley. The latter had signed the death warrant of King Charles I.

In 1663 John Myles, the father of Welsh Baptists, settled in the vicinity of Rehoboth in Plymouth Colony. He relocated at the upper end of Warren, sixty miles from Providence, Rhode Island. The Welsh settlements at Swansea, Warren, and Barrington were the smallest Welsh settlements.

Several Huguenots arrived at Boston between 1686 and 1688. They included Gabriel Berson, Paix Cazenaux, James Baudoin, Andre Sigourney, Andre Faneuil, and Louis Allaire. Allan Forbes and P. F. Cadman's *The Boston French, A Collection of Facts and Incidents with Appropriate Illustrations Relating to Some Well Known Homes in New England with Which Are Included Accounts of Several Visits Made by One of the Authors to La Rochelle and to the Home of the American Paul Revere* (New Orleans: Polyanthos, 1971) treats the colonial French as does Mary de Witt Freeland's *The Records of Oxford, Mass. Including Chapters of Sketches and Notes of Nipmuck, Huguenot and English History Accompanied with Biographical Sketches and Notes, 1630-1890 with Manners and Fashions of the Times* and Pierre Belliveau's *French Neutrals in Massachusetts: The Story of the Acadians Rounded up by Soldiers from Massachusetts and Their Captivity in the Bay Colony Province 1755-60* (Boston: Geffen, 1972).

Massachusetts was the first colony as a result of communications and commerce between Boston and the interior towns. King Charles II ordered that a post road link his colonies in North America. It became known as the Old Boston Post Road, which in 1673 extended 250 miles south to New York. It consisted of three forks. The upper route was via Worcester, Springfield, Hartford, and New Haven. The middle route was 225 miles long and had stops at Wethersfield, Berlin, Meriden, Wallingford, and New Haven. The lower route stopped at Saybrook, Guilford, and Branford to New Haven. There was an alternate route via Providence, Scituate, and Coventry, Rhode Island to Norwich and New London, Connecticut. At 270 miles it was the longest route of the three. Travel was enhanced by the stage coach, which Levi Pease introduced as described in Stewart H. Holbrook's *The Old Post Road* (New York: McGraw Hill Book Company, 1962). In 1718 the Rev. William Boyd and his five ship loads of colonists, including his congregation, landed at Boston. Several hundred Scots were sent out to Bangor on Penobscot Bay and to Belfast. The Scots left traces of their origins in the place names of Londonderry, Antrim, and Hillsboro, New Hampshire; Orange County, Vermont; and Coleraine, Massachusetts. The Scots were not well received by the Puritan English.

Germans also settled at Broad Bay, Maine, from 1739 to 1752. Samuel Waldo, a land speculator, had his land surveyed and went to Germany to secure colonists. He retained Sebastian Zouberbuhler, who had experience in other colonies, to take over. A hundred and fifty Germans responded. The Indians in 1746 laid waste and totally destroyed Waldoborough. Only a few Germans escaped. From Waldoboro, Maine, these Germans moved to Pennsylvania. They returned with new recruits from Pennsylvania.

The Massachusetts government noted how Pennsylvania had benefitted by placing German colonists on the frontier. In 1749 the General Court approved four townships for foreign Protestants. They were in the part of Massachusetts that became Maine. Within three years Joseph Crelius imported one hundred and twenty Protestants for each township. More came in 1757. The Germans called their settlement Frankfort, which is Dresden today. Seven families settled at Ashburnham in 1752. The other two settlements withdrew to Braintree, Massachusetts. With the death of Waldo, the Germans found that the title to the land they had purchased from him was much in dispute. They had to buy their lands again but learned that there were even older claims. They removed to the Piedmont of South Carolina in 1770 and 1773 where they settled in Orangeburgh.

Other groups also came. Joseph Carlevale's *Leading Americans of Italian Descent in Massachusetts* (Plymouth: Memorial Press, 1946) and Lee M. Friedman's *Early American Jews: Jews of Massachusetts, New York and Other American Lands* (Cambridge: n.p., 1934) expands on immigrants into the nineteenth century.

Connecticut

The Pilgrims learned about the fertile soil in the Connecticut river valley from the American Indians. Edward Winslow led the exploration party of the region in 1632. The town of Saybrook at the mouth of the river was planted by a party under the leadership of John Winthrop, Jr. John Steele led about fifty persons from Cambridge, Massachusetts to settle across the river at Hartford. The Rev. Thomas Hooker led his entire congregation and their one hundred and sixty head of cattle along the Bay Path to their new home of Hartford in 1641. A group from Dorchester went overland to found Windsor. Settlers from Watertown went by ship to found Wethersfield in 1635. In 1636 the Rev. Thomas Hooker led his entire congregation from the Bay Colony to Wethersfield, Windsor, and Hartford. William Pynchon, who had been a fur trader in the valley, led still another group from Massachusetts to settle Springfield. These river towns became the colony of Connecticut in 1639.

The aftermath of the Pequot War brought forty years of peace and led to the geographical expansion. Within five years, the towns of New Haven in 1638, Guilford in 1639, Milford in 1639, Fairfield in 1639, Stamford in 1640, Greenwich in 1640, and Branford in 1644 were along the coast. Once the gaps among them were filled in, settlement of the upcountry followed.

About 1640 colonists from Devonshire, Dorsetshire, and Yorkshire England, arrived.

The Rev. John Davenport and Theophilus Eaton planted the colony of New Haven in 1638. Donald Lines Jacobus traced the *Families of Ancient New Haven* (Baltimore: Genealogical Publishing Co., 3 vols. 1974). By 1642 people from Connecticut were moving across Long Island Sound to settle at Southold, Long Island.

By 1665 Connecticut had absorbed the New Haven Colony.

In 1754 settlers from Connecticut moved to the Wyoming valley in Pennsylvania.

Connecticut's role in the Revolutionary War was very important. More than 40,000 served. The towns of Danbury, New Haven, Fairfield, Norwalk, New London, and Groton were burned and pillaged by the British.

Cottage industries were widespread in Connecticut. Nutmeggers invented and manufactured

19

a wide array of gadgets, and Yankee peddlers carried them all over the country.

Albert H. Ledoux's *The Franco Americans of Connecticut* (the author, 1977) and Morris Silverman, *Hartford Jews 1659-1970* (Hartford: Connecticut Historical Society, 1970) covered these non-Anglo settlers.

Rhode Island and Providence Plantations

Families established early in the colony which took its name from the shape of the Isle of Rhodes are in John O. Austin's *The Genealogical Dictionary of Rhode Island: Comprising Three Generations of Settlers Who Came before 1690, with Many Families Carried to the Fourth Generation* (Baltimore: Genealogical Publishing Co., 1974) and his *One Hundred and Sixty Allied Families* (Baltimore: Genealogical Publishing Co., 1977) are the major compendia of the earliest colonists.

Groups of Massachusetts rebels founded the first towns in Rhode Island.

In 1635 Roger Williams had been banished from the Bay Colony due to his views on religious toleration and Indian rights. He believed that civil power had no authority to punish religious offenses and insisted on the separation of church and state. He also took the position that the King had no right to grant land that already belonged to the Indians. After spending a season with the Indians, Williams with a few friends from Salem, established Providence. In 1635 Newport was settled. Anne Hutchinson had attracted many listeners to her unorthodox teachings in Massachusetts. Her followers established Portsmouth in 1638 to escape the ire of officials in the Bay Colony. William Coddington and John Clarke also came there. In 1639 Samuel Gorton led his adherents in splitting off from the Portsmouth settlement to found Newport and Warwick in 1643.

The Society of Friends, or the Quakers, found refuge in Rhode Island—notably in the towns of Newport and Providence. They were the most persecuted Christians in Massachusetts. In 1747 the four Massachusetts towns of Bristol, Little Compton, Tiverton, and Warren were annexed by Rhode Island.

Newport was a shipping center. Rum was taken to Africa in exchange for slaves, who in turn, were taken to the West Indies in exchange for molasses, which was taken back to Newport to be made into rum. This was the Triangular Trade.

Because of the sea lane connection with Barbados, members of the Sanford and Borden families located on this sugar island. About 1660, Portsmouth, Rhode Islanders, removed to Plymouth Colony and founded the towns of Tiverton, Little Compton, and Dartmouth. In the second half of the seventeenth century, others removed to Monmouth County, New Jersey. They were the Slocum, Borden, Cook, and Throckmorton families. In the middle of the eighteenth century, the Dickenses and others from New Shoreham migrated to Westchester County, New York. During the French and Indian War, colonists including the Sanfords and Bordens from Portsmouth and New Portsmouth, migrated to Nova Scotia and named their settlement Newport.

In 1686 the proprietors gave encouragement for some four dozen French Huguenots to settle in the Narragansett country. Among them were the Ayrault, Bernon, Caneau, Ginnaldo, Helme, Jerauld, Marney, Targe, and Tourtello families. The French are treated in Elisha R. Potter's *Memoir Concerning the French Settlements and French Settlers in the Colony of Rhode Island* (Baltimore: Genealogical Publishing Co., 1968). They named their settlement Frenchtown. The English forced them to vacate their settlement in 1691 and the settlers scattered elsewhere in Rhode Island and

Massachusetts as well as New York and South Carolina.

Jews arrived in Rhode Island in 1763 and settled at Newport.

During the Revolutionary War loyalists relocated to Nova Scotia and mother England. The Haliburtons were from the former, and the Brentons from the latter. About 1792 the Trim, Rose, Sprague, and Dodge families settled at Islesboro, Maine. Also after the Revolution members of the Sanford, Wilcox, and Hart families moved to Berkshire County, Massachusetts and the Van Rensselaer Patent near Albany, New York. They also settled around Wayne and Ontario counties at Palymra and Rochester.

New Hampshire

Early colonists are treated in Sybil Noyes, C. T. Libby, and Walter Goodwin Davis's *Genealogical Dictionary of Maine and New Hampshire* (Baltimore: Genealogical Publishing Co., 1965), and in Charles H. Pope's *The Pioneers of Maine and New Hampshire 1623 to 1600. A Descriptive List Drawn from Records of the Colonies, Towns, Churches, Courts, and Other Sources* (Baltimore: Genealogical Publishing Co., 1979).

New Hampshire's Atlantic ocean's coastline is only thirteen miles long and is the shortest of all the states. Settlement in New Hampshire dates from 1623 at what is Portsmouth which was located at the only port in the state. Dover farther up the Piscataqua River dates from 1628. Colonists from Norfolk, England, settled Hampton in 1636.

The harsh rule in Massachusetts Bay drove other dissenters north as well. The Rev. John Wheelwright, who had become embroiled in the antinomian controversy of Anne Hutchinson, established Exeter in 1638. Other colonists, arriving directly from England, settled at Rye, Portsmouth, and Dover. They were Anglicans. In 1641, Massachusetts absorbed these settlements. It became a royal province in 1679.

Ulster Scots settled Londonderry, New Hampshire, in the first quarter of the eighteen century.

Col. George Waldo brought a large colony of Palatine Germans in the 1750s.

Huguenots settled in Dresden. Charles E. Allen covered them in *Some Huguenots and Other Early Settlers on the Kennebec in the Present Town of Dresden.* (n .p. 1892).

Vermont

It was not until a century and a score had passed that English colonists made their way into the Green Mountain state. The first English settlement was at Fort Dummer in 1724. Even though Vermont was only 90 miles from the coast, its settlement was quite late when compared to other New England colonies.

The French gave up Vermont in 1763 at the end of the French and Indian War, at which time there were fewer than three hundred settlers in Vermont. There were Scottish Covenanter settlements at Ryegate and Barnet in Caledonia County which in 1764 was still in New York.

One native son stated that "Vermont is the most glorious spot on the face of the globe for a man to be born in, provided he emigrates when he is very young."

Vermont is larger than the other New England states of Massachusetts, Connecticut, New Hampshire, and Rhode Island. It is also bigger than Delaware and Hawaii.

Its eastern border is the Connecticut river; its western border is Lake Champlain. Its early settlers cleared the upper slopes because the uplands basked in the morning sun while fog tended to envelop the valleys below. The valleys were also subject to flooding. During the hot summer season the mosquitoes were worst in the valleys. Frosts and cold weather were more intense in the valleys. The settlers built their barns below their homes to avoid ground level contamination of their well water by livestock.

Between 1760 and 1776 seventy-four new towns were established in Vermont. Most of the settlers had moved once or twice previously. Scottish Covenanters from Glasgow settled Ryegate in 1773.

Vermonters were not in favor of the War of 1812. Vermont farmers exported their grain and potash to Montreal, Canada, via the St. Lawrence. After the war, many Vermonters moved to Ohio for better land. Other New Englanders took their places.

Vermont was the fastest growing state in the union before the War of 1812. It was the slowest one between 1840 and 1850. Vermonters suffered a severe drought on the east side of the mountains in 1800. Those on the west side of the mountains experienced the same in 1805. Rampaging floods in 1811, 1825, and 1830 carried away homes, barns, bridges, mills, and crops. A plague of grasshoppers followed by wheat rust ruined much of the crops in 1811. Soldiers in the War of 1812 introduced spotted fever, which struck down entire families. There were extremely cold summers from 1812 to 1818. In 1816 a foot of snow fell in June, and there were frosts in July and August. The crops were stunted. By 1850 there were one hundred and forty-five thousand Vermonters residing in other states. Between 1850 and 1900 two out of every Vermonters left the state. It was the Vermonter, Horace Greeley, who said to another, "Go west, young man, go west." He was speaking to Josiah B. Grinnell. Grinnell took his advice and moved to Iowa where he founded Grinnell College. Lewis D. Stillwell, *Migration from Vermont* (Montpelier: Vermont Historical Society, 1948) covers the exodus.

Finns came to the Markham Mountain region in Windsor County and to the Equinox Mountain region in Bennington County. The Welsh came to work in the quarries in Rutland County, and the Italians and the Scots were stone cutters southeast of Montpelier.

Lewis D. Stillwell, "Detailed Account of Migrations 1776-1860 of about Eight Thousand Vermonters to the Counties of the United States and Canada," *Proceedings of the Vermont Historical Society,* V, 63-245.

Maine
The English settled at Pemaquid in 1625.

The English Plantation, which became known as Dresden in 1791, was an outpost settled by Huguenots. Included among them were Jean Pochard, Stephen Houdelette, Goulds, and Stilphens.

Of the New England states, Maine suffered more than any other during the Revolutionary War. One of the state Revolutionary War bounty land tracts by Massachusetts was located in Penobscot and Somerset counties. After the war there was rapid settlement, although the lack of access by road was a major hindrance. The British captured several cities in the War of 1812. Maine achieved statehood with the Missouri Comprise in 1820.

The bloodless Aroostock War in Maine in the 1830s pitted the United States against Canada.

There were Germans at Waldoboro. French from Acadia came to Saint John valley after the French and Indian War in 1763. French from Quebec came after the Civil War. See Gary T. Horlacher and Wilford W. Whitaker's *Broad Bay Pioneers, 18th Century German-Speaking Settlers of Present-day Waldoboro, Maine* (Rockland, Maine: Picton, 1998). People from England, and Scandinavia came to work in the shipyards and factories in the nineteenth century. Swedes founded New Sweden, Stockholm, Jemtland, and Linneus about 1870 in the northeastern part of the state.

Chapter Three: The West Indies

British colonization of Bermuda began in 1612, followed by St. Kitts in 1623, Barbados in 1627, Nevis in 1628, and Antigua and Montserrat in 1632. Anguila, Jamaica which Admiral Penn seized in 1655, and Tortola in 1672 were also settled. Half of the ten thousand indentured servants sent to America between 1654 and 1678 went to the West Indies–particularly Barbados and Nevis.

Colonists migrated from the islands in the Caribbean to the mainland and from the mainland to the islands. William Vassal, who was baptized in 1592, came with the Puritans to Massachusetts in 1630. He returned to England in 1646 and two years later went to Barbados where he died in 1657.

The islands are grouped into the Lesser Antilles and the Greater Antilles. The latter were part of the mountainous extension of Central America and, therefore, possessed gold and included the island of Jamaica.

Two reference works are Arnold Talbot Bethell's *Early Settlers of the Bahamas and Colonists of North America and Early Colonists of the Bahamas: A Selection of Records* (Baltimore: Clearfield, 1992) and Natalie A. Zacek's *Settler Society in the English Leeward Islands, 1670-1776.* (Cambridge University Press, 2010).

The American Revolution drove many Loyalists to other parts of the empire. They doubled the population of the Bahamas. Jamaica absorbed ten thousand. Walker T. Dornfest's *Military Loyalists of the American Revolution: Officers and Regiments, 1775-1783* (Jefferson, North Carolina: McFarland & Co., 2011).

James C. Brandow, *Genealogies of Barbados Families from Caribbeana, The Journal of the Barbados Museum and Historical Society* (Baltimore: Genealogical Publishing Co., 1983) contains fifteen thousand persons with many connections with New England and elsewhere on the mainland.

Barbados is rich in records that have been published. Two valuable reference are John C. Hotten's *The Original Lists of Persons of Quality, Emigrants, Religious Exiles, Political Rebels, Serving Men Sold for a Term of Years, Apprentices, Children Stolen, Maidens Pressed, and Others Who Went from Great Britain to the American Plantations, 1600-1700 with Their Ages, the Localities Where They Formerly Lived in the Mother Country, the Names of the Ships in which They Embarked and Other Interesting Particulars, from MSS Preserved in the State Paper Department of Her Majesty's Public Record Office, England* (Baltimore: Genealogical Publishing Co., 1962) and James Brandow's *Omitted Chapters from Hotten's Original List of Persons of Quality and Others Who Went from Great Britain to the American Plantations, 1600-1700, Census Returns, Parish Registers, and Militia Rolls from the Barbados Census 1679/80* (Baltimore: Genealogical Publishing Co., 1982). David L. Kent's *Barbados and America* lists 13,000 Barbadians and about half of the island's 1674 census and the 1715 census (Arlington, Va., n. p.,1981).

Barbados and Scotland connections are treated in David Dobson's *Barbados and Scotland Links 1627-1877* (Baltimore: Clearfield, 2005). It has about 2,500 entries.

Joanne Mcree Saunders has produced three compilations of source material, *Marriages 1643-1800 [and] Baptisms 1637-1800, Barbados Records Wills and Administration*, and *Barbados Church Records 1637-1887.* (Saunders Historical Publications: Houston, Texas, 1979).

James C. Brandon's *Genealogies of Barbados Families* (Baltimore, Md.: Genealogical Publishing Co., 1982) illustrates the inter-colonial migrations listing Joseph and Anne Borden, Joseph Harbin, Tobias and Lucy Frere, Constant Silvester, the Rev. Dudley and Ruth Woodbridge, and Davenport, White-Vassal, and Maverick who came from New England.

Jewish settlers in the Caribbean are treated in Mordehay Arbell's *The Jewish Nation of the Caribbean: The Spanish-Portuguese Jewish Settlements in the Caribbean and the Guianas* (New York: Gefen Publishing, 2002) and Natalie A. Zacok's, *Settler Society in the English Leeward Islands, 1670-1776* (Cambridge University Press, 2010.)

Chapter Four: The Middle Colonies

Pioneering in forested North America fell to those in the Middle Colonies. It was they who insured that the United States would not be just a littoral nation but a continental country. The Middle colonies were thickly forested. They were also colder than Mother England.

Corn, peaches, and pork were the foodstuffs that enabled the colonists to survive and multiply. Their essential crop was maize, which would be called corn today. It could produce a thousand fold increase. It yielded four times as much food per unit as did wheat. It also used one-tenth of the seed. Corn required less labor and no tools for harvesting. The corn crop could be gathered over a much longer period of time than wheat. It required no plowing or tilling. It was more easily preserved in the fields in winter by its water proof husks. It also yielded more grain for less labor. Without corn, it would have taken another century for Americans to have reached the Rocky mountains.

The peach tree bore fruit in three years. The plant was most suitable for a mobile population. They required much less care than apple or pear trees. New Englanders preferred mutton as their source of protein, but those in the middle and southern colonies consumed pork. Swine could take care of themselves. They fed off the woods. They required no herders. All of their meat could be used. Their only natural predator was the bear.

The Middle colonies were in the heart of New Sweden. It was the Swedes and the Finns who were axe-wielders and capable of in-forest stabilization. Unlike the British and Dutch, the Swedes and Finns had axes. The settlers in the middle colonies created an inland bulge and extended the frontier into the heartland. The Swedish colonists anglicized their surnames. Bengtsson became Binkston and Pinkston; Gostasson became Eustace, Justice, and Justin; Rimbo became Rambo; and Wallfran became Wallraven.

New York

In 1624 some thirty families, many of whom were Walloons, were the first permanent settlers in New Netherland. Many of them ascended the Hudson river and settled at the post of Fort Orange.

David M. Riker's *Genealogical and Biographical Directory to Persons in New Netherland from 1613 to 1674* (Salem: Higginson Books, 1999) and Edwin R. Purple's *Contributions to the History of Ancient Families of New Netherland and New York* (N.Y.: privately printed, 1881) are good genealogical compendia.

The tradition of English living among the Dutch stems from the Pilgrims who settled at Leiden. In New Netherland the same tolerant society allowed for religious diversity. In 1640, the English established Southold and Southampton on Long Island, New York.

Lady Deborah Moody was a London aristocrat who converted to Anabaptism. She was in her fifties when she fled to New England. She insisted that baptism be withheld from a person until he or she understood it. Salem threatened to banish her unless she renounced her radical faith. Accordingly, she and her followers removed to Gravesend on the southwestern tip of Long Island in New Netherland. Anne Hutchinson wanted to do away with the doctrine of original sin. She accepted the invitation to settle in New Amsterdam at Pelham Bay in the Bronx. She, six of her children, and nine others died in the massacre at that outpost. The Rev. Francis Doughty was forced out of his vicarage in Gloucestershire and came to Massachusetts Bay where he preached that Abraham's children should have been baptized. His theology caused him to fall out of favor with the Puritans, so he too headed for Long Island where he received a generous land grant. He survived a vicious Indian attack but opted to relocate within Manhattan. Quakers fled Old England for New England, where they met harsh resistance. Mary Dyer was executed. Many Quakers moved to New Netherland and proselytized among the English towns on Long Island.

Fur traders and land speculators dissuaded colonists from settling in the colony of New York. The fur traders looked upon farmers as blocking the trade for pelts with the Iroquois via the Hudson River Valley and westward in the Mohawk River Valley. Albany never experienced a growth in population. The royal grants were vast and sought to replicate a manorial system. Land lords acquired manors of millions of acres such as the Hardenbergh patent. Others such as Cortland were smaller. The landholders were willing to lease their holdings. Small farmers opted to go to other colonies instead, where they could purchase land.

In 1654, twenty-three Sephardic Jews arrived. They were refugees from the Dutch colony of Recife, Brazil. The Portuguese had conquered the colony in that year, and the Jews feared the Portuguese Inquisition. They had left Brazil and intended to go to Holland, but they lacked the financial resources for the longer journey.

In 1678, Huguenots from Frankenthal and Mutterstadt in the Rhineland Pfalz arrived. Among them were Louis DuBois, Christian Deyo, Abraham Hasbrook, Louis Perrier, Anthony Crispel, Hugo Frere, and Simon Le Fevre. They named their settlement New Paltz. Ralph Le Fevre's *History of New Pfalz, New York and Its Old Families, from 1678 to 1820 Including the Huguenot Pioneers and Others Who Settled in New Pfalz Previous to the Revolution* (Bowie, Md.: Heritage Books, 1992) treats the subject of the Huguenot families. See also Paula W. Carlo's *Huguenot Refugees in Colonial New York: Becoming American in the Hudson Valley* (Portland, Oregon: Sussex Academic Press, 2005).

In 1686, Huguenots from the West Indies arrived. Others from England joined them. They named their settlement in Westchester County New Rochelle. See Morgan H. Seacord's *Biographical Sketches and Index of the Huguenot Settlers of New Rochelle, 1687-1776 (N.Y., ca. 1941).* Edmond B. O'Callaghan's *The Register of New Netherland, 1626-1674* (New York: J. Munsell, 1911) treats the entire colony which included New Jersey and Delaware.

In 1708, more than fifty Palatines led by The Rev. Joshua Kocherthal made their way down the Rhine river to Holland, where English ships carried them to London before going to New York. They landed at Flushing and spent the winter in New York City. In the spring they went fifty-five miles up the Hudson to Newburg on the west bank. There were fifty-five in the initial party. Their numbers grew to three thousand. They were to provide tar, pitch, and masts for the English navy. The experiment ended in disaster by 1712. Some of them made their way to the Schoharie River Valley. By 1721, they were finally vested in free lands along the Mohawk, where they founded the towns of Palatine and Stone Arabia. In 1723 they founded Herkimer. The most disenchanted made their way to the Tulpehocken district of Berks County, Pennsylvania. Walter Allen Knittle's *Early Eighteenth Century Palatine Emigration* (Baltimore: Genealogical Publishing Co. 1979) contains 12,000 names. It includes ship lists, Simmendinger's register, and Roman Catholics who returned to Holland. Henry Z. Jones's *The Palatine Families of New York, A Study of the German Immigrants*

28

Who Arrived in Colonial New York in 1710 (the author, 1985) lists eight hundred and forty-seven families. See also his *Even More Families: 18th Century Immigrants to the American Colonies and Their German, Swiss, and Austrian Origins* (Rockport, Maine: Picton Press, 1922) and *More Palatine Families: Some Immigrants to the Middle Colonies 1717-1776 and Their European Origins, Plus New Discoveries on German Families Who Arrived in Colonial New York in 1710.* (Universal City, Calif., 1991).

The governor of New York invited Protestants from Europe to settle in the northern parts of the colony. Groups of Scottish Presbyterians from Argylshire responded. Capt. Lachland Campbell brought 472 Highlanders between 1738 and 1742. They became disenchanted when the land grants promised them did not materialize. Some of them returned to Scotland; others went elsewhere in the colonies. It was not until after the French and Indian War in 1763 and 1764 that their descendants were to receive their lands in Washington County on the Argyle Patent, which contained 47,450 acres. Jennie M. Patten's *The Argyle Patent and Accompanying Documents* (Baltimore: Genealogical Publishing Co., 1965) treats the settlement. There are genealogical notices of the McNaughton, Livingston, Savage, Gillaspie, and Clark families. Other Highlanders who had served in the British army in the war also settled nearby. Many of the ex-soldiers opted to settle in the Mohawk River Valley, where they were strategically situated. They were given grants of 5,000 acres on the condition they settle families proportionately on them. These veterans tended to attract colonists from their home towns. The soldiers were from the 78th Regiment (Fraser Highlanders), the 77th Regiment (Montgomery Highlanders), and the Royal Regiment of Foot (Royal Scots). Sir William Johnston founded the city of Johnston in 1762 and recruited Irish tenant farmers. Many Scots also settled in the area, including a contingent of Roman Catholic MacDonnel Highlanders.

Mieczslaw Haiman, *Poles in New York in the Seventeenth and Eighteenth Centuries* (Chicago: Polish R. C. Union of America, 1938) covers this lesser known ethnic group.

Because the Superintendent of Indian Affairs in the colonies was Sir William Johnston, many Scottish Highlanders came to settle on his Kingsborough Patent as early as 1764. In 1773 he settled 400 from Glengarry, Glenmoriston, Glen Urquhart, and Strath Glass. Each family received 100 acres at the annual rent of £6.3 per annum. After the American Revolution they removed to Glengarry, Canada. They were joined in 1786 by 500 more from Knoydart. Nearly one-third of the battles in the Revolutionary War were in New York.

The Rev. Thomas Clark and three hundred Highland Scots sailed from Newry, Ireland, in 1763 and landed at New York in July 1764. He had received twelve thousand acres for his parishioners. Some of them were lured to South Carolina.

The Holland Land Company obtained territory in western New York. The company extinguished the Indian title of the Seneca in 1797. Three years later the tract had been divided into townships of 6 mile square, and those to be placed on the market were subdivided into 360 acre plots. The purchase price was $2.75 an acre, but it proved to be too high. The company lowered the price to between $1.50 and $2 an acre, eliminated any down payment, and allowed ten years of credit. The response was overwhelming, and the demand caused the price to climb to $5 an acre in 1817. The Genesee Road was extended to Buffalo between 1798 and 1803. Another route was from Niagara through Batavia to Genesee. A third route went from Buffalo to Erie. Joseph Ellicott of the Holland Land Company allowed farmers to pay for their land by road work.

The Holland Land Company advertised heavily in New England in order to populate its holdings. In 1797 one traveler counted 500 wagons passing through Albany daily.

New York issued its Revolutionary War bounty land grants in the Finger Lakes region in the central part of the state in the counties of Cayuga, Cortland, Onondaga, Seneca, and parts of Oswego, Schuyler, Tompkins, and Wayne counties. Approximately twenty-five thousand people were living in the Holland Land Company purchase by 1812. More than 200,000 people lived in western New York and at least two-thirds came from Massachusetts, Rhode Island, and Connecticut.

From western New York the Mohawk River, rising 578 feet above sea level, led to the Great Lakes. New York authorized the Erie Canal in 1817. It opened in 1825 and paid for itself within nine years. It enabled New York City to become the largest city in the nation. The canal lowered freight charges and enabled crops from the west to reach the port.

The Norwegians in New York are discussed in Andrew N. Rygg's *Norwegians in New York, 1825-1925* (Brooklyn, N.Y. Norwegian News Company, 1941).

Nineteenth century Germans in the Big Apple are the subject of Stanley Nadel's *Little Germany: Ethnicity, Religion, and Class in Yew York City 1845-80* (Urbana: University of Illinois Press, 1990).

New Jersey

The only successful Dutch settlement in New Jersey was Bergen.

In 1655 the Dutch took over New Sweden, and the English took New Netherland over in 1664. Lord John Berkeley and Sir George Carteret were granted the area between the Delaware and Hudson Rivers and opened the doors to settlers, who came in great numbers.

After the English assumed control of New Netherland, settlers from the Piscataqua in New Hampshire, Cape Cod, and Long Island established the towns of Woodbridge and Piscataway in Middlesex County.

Speculators from Barbados purchased large tracts in what became known as New Barbados from 1667 to 1670.

Settlers from Long Island founded Elizabethtown in 1662. They included John Baker of New York, John Ogden from Southampton, John Bayley from Jamaica, and Luke Watson from Jamaica.

New Jersey initially consisted of two parts: East Jersey and West Jersey. West Jersey was the southern part and was closely allied with Pennsylvania. It was mostly Quaker.

From Newbury, Massachusetts in 1666 came a group headed by Daniel Pierce. John Pike and Andrew Tappan were with him. The nine signatories to the confirmation deed for Woodbridge were Daniel Pierce, Joshua Pierce, John Pike, John Bishop, Henry Jacquees, and Hugh March from Newbury. From Haverhill came Stephen Kent. From Barnstable came John Smith. Robert Dennis was from Yarmouth. Three months later they sold one-third of their holdings to John Martin, Charles Gilman, Hugh Dunn, and Hopewell Hull from New Hampshire. They called their settlement Piscataway.

In what became Monmouth County the patentees were from Gravesend, Long Island. They included John Browne, James Grover, Richard Stout, Samuel Spicer, Richard Gibbons, John Tilton, and William Goulding. Some came from the eastern end of Long Island.

East Jersey was the northern part and was closely allied with the Dutch. Settlers came from New York City, Kings County, and the Hudson River Valley.

Puritans from the New Haven Colony towns of Milford, Guilford, and Branford, Connecticut, settled Newark in 1665. Robert Treat, Jasper Crane, and Abraham Pierson were the three founders.

In 1667 William Sandford, Nathaniel Kingsland, Samuel Moore, Michael Smith, Lewis Morris, and John Palmer acquired 15,000 acres in Bergen County. They were Barbadians.

In 1675 a ship load of Friends from England began settling in West Jersey at Salem. Their settlement was the first permanent English speaking settlement in New Jersey. The colony's founder, John Fenwick, came on the *Griffin*. By 1681 some fourteen hundred were in West Jersey including the Finns and Swedes, which the colony absorbed.

In 1682 William Penn acquired East Jersey.

Between 1683 and 1685 Scots settled at the port of Perth Amboy, named for the Earl of Perth. By 1720, there were three thousand Scots in New Jersey. They were predominantly Calvinists from Edinburgh, Montrose, Aberdeen, and Kelso.

In the 1690s there was a significant migration of eastern Long Islanders to Cape May. In the 1730s others from the same area came to Morris County. In 1697 Fairfield was settled by colonists from Fairfield, Connecticut.

In 1702 New Jersey became a royal province governed by the governor of New York, but the proprietors of New Jersey retained their control of the land.

Fifteen to twenty Welsh families from Pembrokeshire, after sojourning in Pennsylvania, relocated in New Castle County in 1705.

Ulrich Simmendinger, *True and Authentic Register of Persons ... Who in the Year 1709 ... Journeyed from Germany to America* (Baltimore: Genealogical Publishing Co., 1984) is devoted to the immigrant Germans of New Jersey.

There were some five thousand Loyalists who left New Jersey after the Revolutionary War. They made their way via New York to Canada–especially Nova Scotia–or to England.

Adrian C. Leiby's *The Early Dutch and Swedish Settlers of New Jersey* (Princeton, N.J. 1964) focuses on the seventeenth century. *Huguenot Settlement of Schraalenburg, the History of Bergenfield, New Jersey* (Bergenfield Free Public Library, 1964) covers the French Huguenots as do David D. Demarest's *The Huguenots on the Hackensack* and Albert F. Koehler's *The Huguenots or Early French in New Jersey* (Baltimore: Genealogical Publishing Co., 2007).

Other seminal works on New Jersey pioneers include: Theodore F. Chambers, *The Early Germans of New Jersey: Their History, Churches, and Genealogies* (Baltimore: Genealogical Publishing Co, 1969).Joseph W. Carlevale, *Americans of Italian Descent in New Jersey* (Clifton, N. J. : North Jersey Press, 1950) focuses on the Italians.Joseph Brandes, *Immigrants to Freedom*; *Jewish Communities in Rural New Jersey* (University of Pennsylvania Press, 1971) relates the Jewish role in New Jersey.

Pennsylvania

The Dutch were the first Europeans in Pennsylvania and were unchallenged until 1638 when the Swedes began their settlement. The Dutch from New Amsterdam conquered the area in 1655. Amandus Johnson's *The Swedish Settlements on the Delaware 1638-64* (Baltimore: Genealogical Publishing Co, 1969) and Evert A. Louhi's *The First Permanent Settlements in Pennsylvania, Delaware, West New Jersey, and Eastern Part of Maryland* (Humanity Press, 1925) covers Scandinavians on the Atlantic and Chesapeake coastlines.

Jacob R. Marcus's *Early American Jewry* (Philadelphia: Jewish Publication Society of

America, 1953) covers Pennsylvania.

Between 1674 and 1681 during the administration of Governor Edmund Andros, a number of land patents in the area were issued. The tracts adjoined each other. A little English colony developed several years before the arrival of William Penn as described in Wayland F. Dunaway's "The English Settlers in Colonial Pennsylvania,"*Pennsylvania Magazine of History and Biography,* LII (1928) 317-41.

The Quakers believed in religious toleration and equality of everyone before God. Sixty ships arrived in Pennsylvania in 1683. Most of the early settlers arriving were English Quakers. Albert C. Myers treated the Irish Quakers in *Immigration of the Irish Quakers into Pennsylvania 1682 -1750 with Their Early History in Ireland* (Baltimore: Genealogical Publishing Co., 1978). By 1700 there were some two hundred Anglicans who were members of Christ Church. There were three Pennsylvania Baptist congregations by 1700 among the English and Welsh. English Presbyterians from Barbados came in 1698.

William Penn had been granted the area west of the Delaware River by 1682. His colony was the twelfth one out of the original thirteen to be planted. It was the only one with no coast on the Atlantic Ocean. His first settlers were primarily Quakers from England and Wales who settled Philadelphia, Chester, and Bucks counties. They are treated in Walter Lee Sheppard's *The Welcome Claimants: Proved, Disproved, and Doubtful with an Account of Some of Their Descendants.* (Baltimore: Genealogical Publishing Co., 1970). Albert Cook Meyers' *Quaker Arrivals at Philadelphia, 1782-1750. Being a List of Certificates of Removal Received at the Philadelphia Monthly Meeting of Friends* (Baltimore: Genealogical Publishing Co., 1978) contains much useful data about their last residences before coming to the New World. Philadelphia was laid out in 1682 and became the largest city in the colonies. By the time of the Revolution it was the second largest English-speaking city in the world. Only London was larger. Between 1682 and 1685, ninety shiploads of Quakers arrived. By 1750 the Quakers were the third largest religious denomination in America.

There was a Welsh settlement of Quakers that lay within parts of Montgomery, Chester, and Delaware counties. The initial settlements were at Merion and Haverford in 1682. William L. Hull's *William Penn and the Dutch Quakers Migration to Pennsylvania* (Baltimore: Genealogical Publishing Co.; 1970) treats the German Quakers. Welsh settlement occurred at Gwynedd Township in Montgomery County. Welsh Baptists from Llanddewi, Radnorshire, established the Pennepek Church in 1688. The Welsh are treated in Charles H. Browning's, *Welsh Settlement of Pennsylvania* (Baltimore: Genealogical Publishing Co., 1967), Thomas Glenn's *Merion in the Welsh Tract,* (Baltimore: Genealogical Publishing Co., 1967), and his *Welsh Founders of Pennsylvania* (Baltimore: Genealogical Publishing Co., 1970).

Chessman A. Herrick's *White Servitude in Pennsylvania. Indentured and Redemption Labor in Colony and Commonwealth* (Philadelphia,: J. J. McVey, 1926) covers Penn's aversion to African slaves and the colony's need for free labor. Herrick explains the causes and conditions before 1700.

Colonists from New England accounted for the most numerous of migrants from other colonies. The Rev. Thomas Dungan and his family of Rhode Island came to Bristol in Bucks County. His Baptist congregation was predominantly Welsh and English. Benjamin Franklin came from Massachusetts, and Jared Ingersoll from Connecticut.

The Susquehanna Company was formed by Nutmeggers pouring into the Wyoming Valley in Westmoreland County. More than nineteen hundred resided there in 1774.

The term, "Pennsylvania Dutch," connotes the Germans who came to colonial Pennsylvania. Most of them came from Alsace, Wuerttemberg, Baden, and the Rhineland. They applied the term to themselves. Huguenots and Swiss were also styled with the same label. Besides Germany, Germans from Austria, Belgium, the Netherlands, and Switzerland also comprised the Pennsylvania Dutch. At least 80,000 or as many as 100,000 Germans came to colonial North America.

William Penn visited Germany from 1671 to 1677 to propagate his Quaker faith. Germans began arriving in 1683 in Pennsylvania. They settled Germantown north of Philadelphia. Franz Daniel Pastorius led 13 Mennonite and Quaker families from Krefeld. Johann Kelpius led a group of German mystics and formed a brotherhood on Wisshickon Creek near Philadelphia in 1694. Samuel Pennypacker's *The Settlement of Germantown, Pennsylvania, and the German Immigration to North America* (Philadelphia: Pennsylvania German Society, 1899) is the best source on the Germans. Peter Becker led German Baptist "Dunkers" to Germantown in 1719. A decade later their founder, Alexander Mack, with others joined them. Members of the Schwenkfelder sect from Silesia settled in Montgomery County, Pennsylvania, in 1732. The port of Philadelphia began requiring officials to keep records of foreigners. The Germans arrived in two waves. The first was between 1708 and 1720; the second was between 1720 and 1750. The Schwenkfelder families are treated in Samuel K. Brecht's *The Genealogical Record of the Schwenkfelder Families* (New York, 1923).

Frank R. Diffenderfer's *The German Immigration into Pennsylvania through the Port of Philadelphia from 1700 to 1775 and the Redemptioners* (Baltimore, Genealogical Publishing Co., 1979) and Ralph B. Strassburger's *Pennsylvania German Pioneers* (Baltimore: Genealogical Publishing Company, 1966) listing 83,000 immigrants, are excellent in their scholarship. Male Germans sixteen years and older were required to take the oath of allegiance. Don Yoder's *Pennsylvania German Immigrants 1709-1786,* (Baltimore: Genealogical Publishing Co., 1980) and his *Rhineland Emigrant Lists of German Settlers in Colonial America* (Baltimore: Genealogical Publishing Co., 1981) are more recent sources. Frank Eshleman, *Historic Background and Annals of the Swiss and German Pioneers of Southeastern Pennsylvania* (Baltimore: Genealogical Publishing Co.,1969) is another notable reference works. Others appear in *Master Index to the Emigrants Documents in the Published Works of Annette Kunselman Burgert* and in Werner Hacker's *Eighteenth Century Register of Emigrants from Southwestern Germany to America and Other Countries* (Apollo, Pa. Closson Press, 1994).

French Huguenots also came to Pennsylvania, but they had no central settlement. There were more than eight thousand. Ammon Stapleton, *Memorials of the Huguenots in America with Special Reference to Their Emigration to Pennsylvania* (Baltimore: Genealogical Publishing Co., 1969) and Gregory A. Wood's *The French Presence in Maryland, 1624-1800* (Gateway Press, 1978) complement the others.

Levi Oscar Kuhns' *The German and Swiss Settlements of Colonial Pennsylvania.* (New York: AMS Press, 1971), Julius F. Sachse's *The German Pietists of Provincial Pennsylvania 1694-1700* (New York: AMS Press, 1971), and *The German Sectarians of Pennsylvania 1708-1800* (New York: AMS Press, 1971) are also essential works.

The Amish settled in Lancaster County in the early eighteenth century. *Montbellard Mennonite Church Register 1750-1958, A Sourcebook for Amish Mennonite History and Genealogy* (2 vols., Goshen, Indiana: Mennonite Historical Society, 2015) is quite noteworthy.

In 1709 Mennonites from Switzerland settled along Pequea Creek in Lancaster County. Hundreds joined them. By 1730 there were a number of colonists in Lancaster County. They did not have any navigable waterway to bring their produce to the markets in the east. Accordingly, they petitioned that a road be built for this purpose. Construction of the sixty-three mile road was completed in 1741. It became known as the Great Philadelphia Wagon Road. Elmer Smith, J. G. Stewart, and M. E. Kyger's *The Pennsylvania Germans of the Shenandoah Valley* (Allentown: Pennsylvania German Folklore Society, 1964) covers the expansion of the colonial Germans.

In the French and Indian War, Braddock's Road became the first one to penetrate the Appalachian Mountains. It was constructed to allow the supplies for his advancing troops in the interior. It ran through Philadelphia, Lancaster, Harrisburg, Carlisle, Chambersburg, Fort Littleton, Fort Bedford, Fort Ligonier, and Fort Duquesne (Pittsburg). Forbes Road ran through Philadelphia, Lancaster, York, Gettysburg, Hagerstown, Fort Cumberland, Fort Necessity, and Fort Duquesne.

In 1742 Nikolaus Ludwig, Graf von Zinzendorf und Pottendorf, founded the Moravian settlement of Bethlehem, Pennsylvania. Moravian Bishop August G. Spangenberg estimated that there were a hundred thousand German speaking colonists in Pennsylvania.

The Ulster Scots were not inclined to immigrate to New England where ethnic differences and theology discriminated against them. Moreover, there was little vacant land available there. New York favored large land owners. New Jersey did not favor indentured servants, which was one of the techniques the Ulster Scots used to obtain trans-Atlantic passage. In Virginia and Maryland, the Anglican Church was the state church. North Carolina's outer banks constituted a geographical barrier that prevented ships from landing. The tidewater south was based on a slave labor economy so there few opportunities for finding employment. John W. Dinsmore's *The Scotch-Irish in America, Their History, Traits, Institutions and Influences as Illustrated in the Early Settlers of Western Pennsylvania and Their Descendants* (Chicago, 1906) and Wayland F. Dunaway's *The Scotch-Irish of Colonial Pennsylvania* (Baltimore: Genealogical Publishing Company, 1981) discusses the Scots who came from Ireland. *Scotch Irish Pioneers in Ulster and America* (Baltimore: Clearfield, 2001) covers New England, Pennsylvania, South Carolina, and Maryland. The term Scotch-Irish does not indicate the offspring of a Scot and an Irish union but connotes any Scot who lived in Ulster Plantation in Ireland.

Pennsylvania, however, was held in high regard by the Scots-Irish. The Secretary of the Province was one of their own, James Logan. He named his large tract of land in Lancaster County Donegal. They were well represented in Cumberland, Franklin, Northumberland, Huntingdon, Bedford, Westmoreland, Washington, Fayette, and Allegheny counties.

There were four waves of the Ulster Scots arrivals. The first was 1717 to 1718 due to rent racking in Ulster. The second was 1725 to 1729 and was also due to rent racking and rising taxes. In 1740, four hundred thousand settlers in Ulster died in epidemics, and survivors sought to escape. A drought in 1754 to1755 was the fourth period.

New Castle, Delaware, and Philadelphia, Pennsylvania, were important ports of arrival. By the end of the colonial period, one-third of the colony was Scots-Irish. They served as a buffer with the Indians, and by the 1730s were at the foothills of the Alleghenies. It was not until 1768, however, that the western part of Pennsylvania was open for settlement.

Jews arrived in 1745. There was a sudden increase in their numbers when the British took over New York City in 1776. In 1795 the largest Ashkenazi synagogue in the western hemisphere was founded in Philadelphia.

By 1751 the city of Philadelphia had a population of 14,000, which was a fantastic increase in 68 years. In 1753 Christopher Gist went from the Potomac river to Redstone creek in Pennsylvania. He persuaded eleven families to join him. By 1760 there were 146 cabins at Fort Pitt.

During the second half of the eighteenth century the expanding frontier of Pennsylvania caused the farmers in the west to send their products to market and have manufactured goods shipped out to them. The mode of transport became the Conestoga wagon built by the Germans and Swiss for the overland freight hauling. Its original flatbed had its floor lowered and slopped toward the center. The Conestoga wagon was 26 feet long and 11 feet high capable of carrying several tons. The wheels were enlarged so that the prairie schooner could cross rivers and streams easier. The wagon makers added a large canvas tarp on wooden hoops to protect people and goods. Ten or twelve horses or oxen were required to pull the wagon. A Conestoga wagon covered about five miles a day.

Between 1756 and 1765 there were twenty-nine new towns in Pennsylvania, which was more than in the previous seventy-five years.

The boundary dispute with Maryland was finally settled by the Mason and Dixon survey in 1763 and 1767 and served to stabilize property lines.

Connecticut and Pennsylvania were locked in a dispute for the ownership of the Wyoming Valley. After the French and Indian War, Connecticut sent out settlers to occupy the land in the vicinity of present-day Scranton and Wilkes-Barre. They were from Windham County, Connecticut. The Pennamite war between 1769 and 1775 pitted settlers in the Wyoming Valley from Connecticut against those from Pennsylvania. By the decree of Trenton in 1782, Pennsylvania gained control of the area, and Connecticut finally acknowledged the same in 1784.

Joseph A. Borkowski's *Prominent Polish Pioneers of the United States of America, 1770-1790* (Pittsburgh: Polish Falcons, 1975) concerns the Poles in the early years of the nation, including Pennsylvania. Miecislaus Haiman's *Polish Pioneers of Pennsylvania* (San Francisco, R. & E. Research Association) does as well.

Virginians and Marylanders furnished a number of migrants to Pennsylvania after the French and Indian war. They settled in Fayette, Greene, Washington, and Westmoreland counties. Some were Scottish and a few were Germans, but the majority were of English stock. Quakers from Berkeley and Frederick counties, Virginia, migrated to Pennsylvania where the evil of slavery did not exist.

The West Indies furnished its share of migrants to Pennsylvania. Isaac Norris, Jonathan Dickinson, and Samuel Carpenter came from Jamaica and Barbados. Anglo-Irish Quakers were also significant in colonizing Pennsylvania.

Parts of Armstrong, Butler, Lawrence, Forest, Venango, and Warren counties were set aside for state Revolutionary War bounty lands for Pennsylvanians.

In western Pennsylvania after the Revolutionary War "seed was so scarce that on one occasion when a hen had eaten some melon seeds placed in the sun to dry, the owner cut open the chicken's crop, extracted the seeds, and then sewed up the gash because she could not afford to lose the hen." Between 1798 and 1815, government repression in Ireland, heavy maritime taxation in the Napoleonic wars, and a severe economic depression after the battle of Waterloo accounted for the greatest number of Scots-Irish to settle in southwestern Pennsylvania. The overlapping claim to southwestern Pennsylvania and Virginia was resolved in 1785. In 1792 Pennsylvania bought the Erie Triangle in order to gain a port on Lake Erie. By 1798 there were seventy-five thousand settlers along the Monongahela, Allegheny, and Ohio Rivers. By 1810 there were two hundred ten thousand in the area. They were joined by Virginians who followed the waterways of the Monongahela and Youghiogheny. From eastern Pennsylvania, Delaware, and Maryland, Scots-Irish immigrants followed the Braddock and Forbes roads.

In 1786 German Mennonites from Pennsylvania began to immigrate to Ontario, Canada, and continued doing so in the first decade of the nineteenth century.

By 1811 steamboat travel was underway between Pittsburgh and New Orleans. By 1834 railroad and canal traffic linked Philadelphia and Pittsburgh. Thousands of immigrants took advantage of the improvements in order to move into the interior.

Delaware

Delaware was part of the colony of New Sweden from 1638 to 1655, when the Dutch gained control. The Swedes called their settlement Fort Christina in 1638, which is Wilmington today. It was named in honor of the queen of Sweden. Many of the colonists were Finns. In 1651 Peter Stuyvesant built and garrisoned a fort on the Delaware a few miles below Christina at Sand Hook called Fort Casimir. The Swedes seized the fort in 1654 and renamed it Fort Trinity. The next year the Dutch took the fort and annexed it to New Netherland. There were nine hundred settlers and soldiers there between 1657 and 1663. Pieter Cornelisz Plockhoy settled forty Mennonites at Whorekill in 1663. When the English seized the area in 1664, they slaughtered the Mennonites. The area was attached to the dominion of James, Duke of York, and Albany. The second period of Dutch rule was from 1673 to 1674, and English colonists from Maryland and Virginia arrived. Among them were the Manloves, Irons, Paradees, and Rawlings in Kent County. From 1680 it was under the jurisdiction of William Penn.

Delaware's boundary with neighboring colonies posed difficulties. It was not until 1769 that the final boundary between Delaware and Maryland was settled. The survey line had been run by Charles Mason and Jeremiah Dixon from 1763 to 1768.

Residents in the land between the Nanticoke and Indian rivers would be in Maryland records. Most of the early settlers of Sussex and Kent Countyies were Quakers. The earliest monthly meeting with extant records was Duck Creek from 1705, which was part of the Chester County, Pennsylvania, meeting, thereby accounting for the presence of so many Chester County families in Kent County.

Welsh Baptists settled in Pencader Hundred in New Castle County.

Maryland

As the second Tidewater colony, Maryland benefitted immensely by the experience in Virginia. The colony was granted in 1632 to George Calvert, Lord Baltimore, who was a prominent English Roman Catholic. He sought a New World haven for persecuted fellow church members. The *Ark* and the *Dove* brought the first colonists to Maryland. There were about twenty Roman Catholics and a hundred and fifty Protestants. The first settlement was at St. Mary's on the St. George River in 1634. Located on high ground, Lord Baltimore had purchased the land from the Indians thereby enjoying freedom from disease and Indian attack.

George E. and Donna Valley Russell trace *The Ark and Dove Adventurers*. (Baltimore: Genealogical Publishing Co., 2005). Acadians from Nova Scotia are treated in Gregory A. Wood's *A Guide to Acadians in Maryland in the Eighteenth and Nineteenth Centuries* (Wheatland, Georgia, Gateway Press, 1995) and his *The French Presence in Maryland, 1574-1800* (Baltimore: Genealogical Publishing Co., 1978.)

The colonists borrowed the cash crop of tobacco, which had saved the existence of Virginia. Puritans settled in Anne Arundel County. A number of them were from Isle of Wight and Nansemond counties, Virginia. They included William Ayres, Robert Brasseur, Henry Bradley, Edward Darcy, Thomas Jordan, Epaphroditus Lawson, Cornelius Lloyd, Edward Lloyd, Thomas Meers, John Norwood, Henry Sewell, Oliver Spry, and Nathaniel Utie. Many of these Puritans became Quakers. The eastern shore also had Quakers in Talbot County. Prior to 1699 forty-two thousand colonists arrived in Maryland. Harry W. Newman's *To Maryland from Overseas: A Complete Digest of the Jacobite Loyalists Sold into White Slavery in Maryland and the British and Continental Background of Approximately 1400 Maryland Settlers from 1634 to the Early Federal Period with Source Documentation* (Baltimore: Genealogical Publishing Co., 1985) is based on land records. Carson Gibbs and Gust Skordas' A *Supplement to the Early Settlers of Maryland Comprising 8680 Entries Correcting Omissions and Errors in Gust Skordas The Early Settlers of Maryland* (Baltimore: Genealogical Publishing Co., 1985.) Gust Skordas, *Early Settlers of Maryland 1679-1783* and Peter Wilson Coldham's *Settlers of Maryland 1679-1783* (Baltimore: Genealogical Publishing Co., 5 vols. 1995-2002) name both immigrants and early settlers.

The migration of Presbyterian ministers began with the Rev. Francis Makemie who founded a congregation at Snow Hill in 1683.

Hundreds of transported Jacobites landed at Oxford, Maryland, in 1746. Ninian Beale, a native of Largo, Fife, Scotland, was one of the Scots banished by Oliver Cromwell for his part in the battle of Dunbar. He was shipped to Barbados. In 1652 he came to Maryland where he named his plantation tract Fife's Largo.

The Germans settled in the western part of Maryland. Moravians from Pennsylvania removed to Graceham, Maryland. Dieter Cunz's *The Maryland Germans, A History* (Port Washington: Kennikat, 1972), Edward T. Schultz, *First Settlement of Germans in Maryland* (Frederick, Md.: Frederick County Historical Society, 1896), and Daniel W. Neal, *The Pennsylvania Germans in the Settlement of Maryland* (Baltimore, Md. Genealogical Publishing Co., 1975) treat the Germans.

Quakers settled in the Monocacy Valley by 1729. The Friends were in Salem County, New Jersey and the Nottingham region of Chester County, Pennsylvania.

Maryland sought to lure German and Ulster Scots families from neighboring Pennsylvania by offering 200 acres free to those who would settle between the Potomac and Susquehanna Rivers. They were also exempt from paying quit rents for three years.

During the French and Indian War about a thousand French residents of Nova Scotia were deported to Baltimore, Maryland in 1755.

Race riots in Santo Domingo drove a thousand French to Baltimore in 1793. Workers on digging the canals in the state brought many, many Irish to the state between 1817 and 1847.

The 15,000 Maryland Roman Catholics who migrated to Perry County, Missouri, some of whom later removed to Texas, are covered in Timothy O'Rourke, *Maryland Catholics on the*

Frontier, the Missouri and Texas Settlements (Parsons, Kansas: Breffny Press, *1973*).
    Marylanders migrated westward in significant numbers. Henry C. Peden
has studied many of these families: *More Marylanders to Kentucky 1778-1828* (Family Line
Publications 1998), *Marylanders to Tennessee 1775-1830* (Lewes, Md. : Colonial Roots, 2004),
Marylanders to Carolina: Migrations of Marylanders to North and South Carolina prior to 1800
(Westminister, Md,: Family Line Publications 1994.) *More Marylanders to Ohio and Indiana;
Migrations prior to 1835* (Lewes, Maryland.: Colonial Roots, 2006).

Chapter Five: The Southern Colonies

The original southern colonies differed from their British neighbors to the North in at least five important respects. In terms of religious background, the founders and settlers of the southern colonies were loyal to the established Church of England (Anglican), whereas 17th-century New England and much of the Middle Colonies were dissenters. Secondly, while all colonists required the New World to afford them an economic livelihood, it is probably fair to say that the settlers of the South Atlantic Coast, who after all were not religious dissenters, were more purely materialistic and less communitarian than their New England or even Middle Colony counterparts. It was just as well that southern pioneers were disinterested in establishing tightly knit communities, thirdly, for arable land in the South was abundant and relatively easy to come by–as witnessed by the vast holdings accumulated by the Carters and Byrds in Virginia. Fourth, the South also enjoyed a far more salubrious climate than New England, something which fostered the growing of staples like tobacco, rice, and cotton. Finally, while most colonies sanctioned African-American slavery–and New England merchants in particular enjoyed large profits from the slave trade–the entire structure of the colonial South's cavalier society was built upon it.

Virginia & West Virginia

William Byrd (1674-1744) wrote that "In the beginning all America was Virginia." He was correct because Virginia was a synonym for any English new world lands on the mainland and that was the definition in usage in his lifetime.

Virginia was the first permanent English colony and was some 3,000 miles away from the Mother Country. It was a privately financed, incorporated stock company that was known as the Virginia Company of London. King James I granted the company its charter in April 1606. Capt. Christopher Newport set sail for Virginia in December 1606 in three ships. They were the *Susan Constant*, the *Godspeed*, and the *Discovery*. The colonists arrived 14 May 1607 at Jamestowne, having been at Martinque, Dominica, Guadeloupe, Nevis, St. Croix, Viegues, Puerto Rico, and Mona & Monica. Its purposes were two-fold: to build a profitable and agricultural company and to hold the area against Spain. Virginia became a royal colony in 1625.

Genealogies of Virginia's first families are covered in John Frederick Dorman's *Adventurers of Purse and Person Virginia 1607-1624/5*, (Baltimore: Genealogical Publishing Co., 2004-2007, 4th ed., 3 volumes.) Martha M. McCartney's *Virginia Immigrants and Adventurers 1607-1635, A Biographical Dictionary* (Baltimore: Genealogical Publishing Co, 2007) broadens coverage, but genealogies are not her focus. Martha McCartney's *Jamestown People to 1800: Landowners, Public Officials, Minorities, and Native Leaders* (Baltimore: Genealogical Publishing Co., 2012) is also quite valuable.

Between 1607 and 1699 eighty-two thousand colonists arrived in Virginia. Perhaps three quarters of them came as indentured servants. Capt. James Davis was with an early settlement at Sagadahoc, Maine. After most of the people sailed back to England, he built a pinnace and sailed for Jamestown in 1607.

David Hackett Fisher's *Bound Away: Virginia and the Westward Movement* (Charlottesville:

University Press, 2000) discusses the expansion of Virginia.

Unfavorable climatic conditions, hostility of the Indians, and the lack of experience were factors that worked against the success of the colony. The London Company was reorganized in 1609. In the spring of 1610, the sixty surviving colonists opted to return to England. At the mouth of James River they encountered Lord de la Warr with four hundred more colonists. They agreed to return to Virginia. In 1611 an additional six hundred fifty colonists arrived. The company's policy of holding land and improvements in common was discontinued in 1616. Land was parceled out among the settlers. Such a policy scattered them along the James and Appomattox rivers.

In 1622 the Indians fell upon the colonists and slew three hundred and fifty of them. Disease and famine also decimated their ranks. In 1624 the King assumed direct control of Virginia and made it a royal colony. Even though a second Indian attack in 1644 resulted in the death of several hundred settlers, the colony quickly rebounded. By 1648 there were fifteen thousand colonists.

During the English civil war, Virginia passed legislation to expel nonconforming preachers in order to suppress Puritanism in Norfolk, Portsmouth, Suffolk, and Isle of Wight. Sir William Berkeley ejected the Puritans. Most of them went to Maryland at present-day Annapolis, which they called Providence. The year 1652 brought the replacement of the governor, Sir William Berkeley, with Richard Bennet. Some scions of affluent Royalist families fled to Virginia. They included Francis Dade, Gorsuch, Col. Joseph Bridger, Sir Henry Chickley, Sir Thomas Lunsford, Col. Philip Honeywood, Col. Henry Norwood, Maj. Richard Fox, Col. Mainwaring Hammond, and Maj. Francis Moryson. The restoration of the monarchy in 1660 led to the concentration of power in the hands of older families and thereby helped create a privileged class. For the support given the royal family, King Charles styled Virginia as the Old Dominion.

Because the governor would not take any action in 1676, Nathaniel Bacon took up arms against the Indians in order to punish those who had been attacking the colonists.

Treatment of the Huguenots may be found in R. A. Brock's *Documents, Chiefly Unpublished, Relating to the Huguenot Emigration to Virginia and to the Settlement at Manakin-town with an Appendix of Genealogies Presenting Data on the Fontaine, Maury, Dupuy, Trabue, Marye, Chastain, Cocke, and Other Families* (Baltimore: Genealogical Publishing Co., 1973) and Priscilla Harriss Cabell's *Turff & Twigg: The French Lands* (Richmond, Va. : the author, 1988) relate the details of the largest Huguenot settlement in the colony.

Huguenots were among the early settlers of Virginia. In the 1620s they settled in Elizabeth City, where they were assigned the task of introducing the culture of grapes. In 1630 others came to Charles River, New Norfolk, Princess Anne, and Isle of Wight counties.

More than six hundred Huguenots arrived in Virginia in 1700 on five ships. The fourth vessel, the *Nassau*, continued farther to New York. In Virginia they settled in King William Parish at Manakintown on the north side of the James in Henrico County in what later became Powhatan and Chesterfield counties. They received 10,000 acres. The settlement was the largest Huguenot settlement in America. They provided a buffer against the Indians, and Manakintown was an area that had already been cleared and allowed Virginia to keep them within her boundaries rather than sharing the colonists with other colonies.

At the end of the seventeenth century a fire at Jamestowne destroyed the capitol, so the seat of government was moved to Williamsburg, where some Huguenots had settled, including the Contess, Marot, and LaPrada families. Coincidental with the removal of the seat, of government was the immigration of more French Huguenots to Manakintown. The settlement included the Agee, Amonet, Chastain, Flournoy, Michaux, Remey, Fontaine, Dupuy, Trabue, Maupin, Soublet, Chastain, Salle, and other families. Even though they were Protestants, the English were somewhat wary of so many of their nation's enemy. Accordingly, a portion of the Huguenots were separated and settled on the freshes of the Mattaponi in King William County. There was much movement between the two French settlements. Among those who settled on the Mattaponi were the Sea, Jeter, Chenault, DeJarnette, Duval, and DeShazo families. Of value is Langston James Goree's *Master Index to the Huguenot, the Biennial Publication of the Huguenot Society Founders of Manakin in the Colony of Virginia and Index to Vestry Book of King William Parish 1701-1750* (Bryan, Texas: Southwest Printing Company, 1986). The society issued its first volume in 1929.

The first advance across the Piedmont into the Shenandoah Valley was via the Rappahannock River Valley rather than the James River Valley due to the influence of Col. Alexander Spotswood. In 1728 he granted several thousand acres to Larkin Chew, the sheriff of Spotsylvania County, and his associates. Virginia promoted settlement of the area in fear of French encirclement and Indian conflicts.

Harry A. Brunk's A *History of Mennonites in Virginia, 1727-1960.* (Verona, Va.: McClure Printing Company, 1959) discusses this German sect.

In 1731, sixteen families settled at Opequon Creek in the Shenandoah Valley. The settlement grew to twenty-five Scots-Irish families, thirteen German families, and twenty-six English or Virginia families. Between 1730 and 1732 there were nine grants for 385,000 acres west of the Blue Ridge Mountains.

From neighboring Pennsylvania, Adam Miller visited Virginia and returned with friends to settle in the Shenandoah Valley between Massanutton mountain and the Blue Ridge. John and Isaac Van Meter, who had lived in Kingston, New York, and Salem, New Jersey, bought land in the Monocacy valley near Frederick, Maryland, in 1726. Virginia offered John Van Meter a grant of 10,000 acres in return for settling the northern part of the valley. If he brought twenty additional families within two years, he would receive 20,000 additional acres.

Virginians like New Englanders clung to the coast but for different reasons. They were tied to the coast by overseas markets for their produce. The Chesapeake Bay was 200 miles long and 30 to 40 miles wide. There were 6,000 miles of shoreline, and forty-eight navigable rivers emptied into it. The growing season was two months longer than in New England.

Typhoid fever, dysentery, and malaria contributed to the deaths of thousands. Prior to the arrivals of Europeans and Africans, the mosquitoes, which acted as insect vectors in transmitting malaria were not present. The death rate made the extended family much more important than in New England where the nuclear family prevailed. There were far more step-members in southern families than in New England.

Initially confined to the James River valley and the Accomack peninsula, Virginians pushed northward to the banks of the York river in the seventeenth century. The soil was equally rich, and the river afforded the means to transport their cash crop of tobacco to market. At the same time, Virginians also occupied the valleys of the Nansemond and Blackwater rivers south of the James.

Between 1649 and 1660 Puritan control of government in England drove thousands of Anglicans to the Chesapeake colonies of Maryland and Virginia. Anglican Cavalier settlers in Virginia included the Byrd, Carter, Culpeper, Custis, Digges, Harrison, Isham, Lee, Madison, Mason,

41

Randolph, Skipwith, and Washington families. Most of them were from the south and west of England. They tended to be younger sons who did not stand to inherit family estates in England. They maintained their political influence by intermarriage. Their close cousinage was likened "to a tangle of fish hooks, so closely interlocked that it is impossible to pick up one without drawing three or four after it." The tables were turned in 1660 with the restoration of Charles II, so Roundheads and Puritans then sought new homes in Maryland and Virginia.

Virginians planted tobacco year after year without resorting to fertilization or crop rotation thus leaving the soil exhausted. Such a decline appeared after three years of cultivation. The colonists then grew several crops of wheat and corn and wore out the land even more. It became necessary to move farther inland to obtain virgin lands. Cultivation of the uplands also brought about significant soil erosion during the heavy summer rains.

The large and detached plantations in Virginia made every family dependent upon its own resources to supply its needs. Mrs. Robert Carter of Nomini Hall reported that in one year the family and servants consumed 27,000 pounds of pork, 20 beeves, 550 bushels of wheat, and 150 gallons of brandy. Her mansion had twenty-eight large fireplaces and required six oxen a day to haul enough firewood to heat the structure in the winter.

There was a population explosion in the Chesapeake between 1645 and 1670 when forty to fifty thousand colonists arrived. Seventy-five percent of them came as indentured servants. Many were unskilled and illiterate. There were four males for every female.

Half of the ten thousand indentured servants to America between 1654 and 1678 were sent to Virginia. Three quarters of them were between the ages of 15 and 24. Three percent were under the age of 15, and less than one percent were over 35 years of age.

It was not until 1683 that Maryland and 1705 that Virginia allowed colonists to purchase new lands farther inland in the Tidewater.

Virginia recruited Scottish Episcopal clergy, beginning with The Rev. David Lindsay in Northumberland County in the 1650s. The Rev. John Munro was at St. John's on the Panumky River in 1658. The Rev. George Robertson was in Bristol Parish by 1693.

The colonial Germans are treated in John Walter Wayland's *The German Element of the Shenandoah Valley of Virginia* (Harrisonburg, Va.,1978), Ulysses S. A. Heavener's *German New River Settlement: Virginia* (Baltimore: Genealogical Publishing Co., 1981), Klaus Wust's *The Virginia Germans* (Charlottesville, Va.: University Press of Virginia, 1969), Klaus Wust's *The Saint Adventurers of the Virginia Frontier, Southern Outposts of Ephrata* (Edinburg,Va. Shenandoah History, 1977), and B. C. Holtzclaw's *Ancestry and Descendants of the Nassau-Siegen Immigrants to Virginia 1714-1750* (Culpeper, Va.: Memorial Foundation of the Germanna Colonies 1978).

In 1714 Christopher von Graffenreidt brought miners from Siegen, Westphalia, to work Governor Spotswood's iron mines. They included the Brumback, Holtzclaw, Kemper, and Hager families. Forty more families arrived in 1718, among whom were the Yeager, Utz, Blankenbaker, and Wilhoite families.

Virginia's colonial government sought settlement in the back country as a buffer against the Indians. Settlement in the area would strengthen Virginia's claim to the territory in the Ohio river valley which the French also claimed. Virginia resorted to granting large tracts of land to speculators. The first grant went to John and Isaac Van Meter for 40,000 acres in Frederick, Clarke, and Jefferson counties. Most of the settlers on this tract were Germans from Pennsylvania. The second large tract was the Beverley Grant in the northern part of Augusta County. It contained more than 118,000 acres. The third tract was the Borden Grant in southern Augusta County and northern Rockbridge County. It encompassed half a million acres. Benjamin Borden had to settle a hundred families on the tract before he received title. He did so by 1739. So many Scots- Irish settled there by 1746 that the tract had become known as the Irish Tract. The southern end of the Valley of Virginia became the second-most populous Ulster Scot settlement in British North America.

The price of land also drew the Germans, Scots-Irish, and English into the Shenandoah Valley. By 1726, settlers had reached Monocacy and Frederick in Maryland. Adam Mueller was the first German to enter the valley in 1727. Jost Hite and eleven other families arrived in 1731 and laid out the town of Winchester. The fear of Indians also prompted settlers to move farther south. Virginia offered cheaper lands in the valley at a cost of ten to twenty shillings per acre.

In 1745 Brethren from Ephrata, Pennsylvania, settled at Mannheim on the New River in Virginia.

The Treaty of Lancaster in 1744 allowed the Indians to use the Great Road to travel to and from New York to the Indian nations in the south.

James Patton, a native of Ulster, Ireland, brought nine shiploads of Scots-Irish to settle on the Beverley Manor in 1745. His son-in-law, John Buchanan, was active in the same scheme. One-third of the valley came from the tidewater counties in northern Virginia. The other two-thirds were almost equally divided between the Germans and Scots-Irish.

Between 1764 and 1775, the Great Wagon Road in the Shenandoah Valley was the most traveled roadway in North America.

In 1775 the distribution of national groups in the Shenandoah valley was:

County	English	Scots-Irish	German
Berkeley	36%	31%	29%
Frederick	40%	25%	30%
Shenandoah	22%	10%	60%
Rockingham	24%	30%	43%
Augusta	20%	58%	19%
Rockbridge	18%	73%	8%

Clearly, ethnic groups tended to cluster. The English predominated in Frederick County; the Scots-Irish in Rockbridge County; and the Germans in Shenandoah County.

After the Revolutionary War there was a considerable migration from New Jersey to Loudoun County, Virginia.

The period after the War of 1812 was one of economic difficulty. The Panic of 1819 saw the prices of agricultural produce fall to new lows. East of the Blue Ridge, continuous cultivation manifested itself by leaving the soil exhausted. Virginians left the commonwealth in such numbers that Virginia dropped to the second most populous state in 1820 and fourth in 1840, while Pennsylvania and New York surged ahead. Land values plummeted. Virginians took losses when they put their farms on the market and moved westward into the Old Northwest and the Old Southwest.

Poles in Virginia are treated in Miecislaus Haiman's *Polish Pioneers of Virginia and Kentucky with Notes on Genealogy of the Sadowsky* (San Francisco: R. E. Research Associates, 1971). The Taliaferro family was the most prolific Italian one. The Italians are treated in Glenn

Weaver's *The Italian Presence in Colonial Virginia* (New York Center for Migration Studies, 1988). Jews are treated in Louis Ginsberg's *Chapters on the Jews of Virginia, 1658-1900.* (Petersburg: n.p., 1969).

North Carolina

North Carolina was the only British colony planted in North America that did not begin with a town. It had few slaves and did not develop a plantation aristocracy.

By 1663 Virginia had established a settlement in Albemarle Sound in the forests and swamps to protect her southern border. The isolated settlement offered safety from tax collectors and reforming ministers. By 1677 there were two thousand five hundred settlers in the area.

James Reeves came to the West Indies in 1635. The following year he settled in Chowan, North Carolina. About 1639 he moved north to Hashamonneck, next to Southhold, Long Island, where he died about 1665. Thomas Osman came to Chowan in 1637. He too eventually pulled out and moved to Southhold, Long Island in 1653.

The first permanent settler in North Carolina was Nathaniel Batts, who had a trading post on the western end of Albemarle Sound. By 1663 the population exceeded five hundred.

By the 1680s settlers began moving south from James River in search of virgin soil to replace the exhausted tobacco farms. By 1729 North Carolina was the most sparsely populated colony with thirty thousand whites and six thousand blacks.

Abraham Kimberley was a Nutmegger from Stratford who settled in North Carolina in Albemarle. After his death his widow and children returned to New England.

William Leveridge, his wife Temperance, and daughter Hannah who came from Albany County, New York, were among the headrights claimed by George Harris for 1,100 acres of land in 1694. Hannah Leverdige married Henry Slade and lived in Bath County.

In 1711 there were appalling massacres along the Chowan and Roanoke rivers. Some twelve hundred Tuscarora Indians fell upon the colonists who had been encroaching upon their lands. In 1712 the forces from South Carolina, numbering thirty white men and three hundred Yamasse, attacked the Indians on the Neuse River. It was not until 1713 that peace returned when Col. James Moore of South Carolina defeated them.

While Virginians were the first to relocate in North Carolina, Rhode Islanders began arriving in 1732. William Borden, a native of Portsmouth, was attracted by the low cost of lumber in the South. He sailed with a group of Quakers from Tiverton, Rhode Island, in 1732. They settled on Core Sound in Carteret County. They named their settlement Newport and the Newport river after their home back in Rhode Island. Borden became one of the south's leading ship builders and employed large numbers of Rhode Islanders who came south in the winter season. He died in 1748. His nephew, Joseph Borden, joined the family in North Carolina. His descendants founded the Borden Milk Company.

William Borden's brother-in-law was Henry Stanton, a Quaker, who bought 1,992 acres in Carteret County in 1721 and moved his family there in 1724. The first Quaker meeting was organized in 1733. His great-grandson was U. S. Secretary of War Edwin M. Stanton.

Christopher Nicholson and his wife, Hannah Rednap, became Quakers in Massachusetts and about 1663 removed to North Carolina to avoid persecution. Henry and Hannah (Baskel) Phelps were from Salem, Massachusetts. She first married Nicholas Phelps, and, upon his death, she married her brother-in-law, Henry Phelps. Her third husband was John Hill. Isaac and Damaris (Shattuck) Page also came from Salem to North Carolina.

In 1704 or 1705 French Huguenots from Manakin Town in Virginia relocated at Bath on Pamlico Sound. More joined them in 1707 or 1708 and settled at the mouth of the Trent River. John Fonvielle was at a vestry in Manakin Town in 1707 and removed to Core Sound, Craven County in 1710. In 1711 following the Indian massacre, the Rev. Claude Philippe de Richebourg and several members of his congregation left Craven County, North Carolina, and settled on the Santee River in South Carolina. About 1736 the area was resettled by Manakin families. Among them were the Calvet, Caillau, Depp, Dupree, and Morrissett families. In New Hanover were Huguenots who came from South Carolina. They included the Poitevints, Befrits, DuBoses, and Bordeaus. The DeRosset family arrived a bit later.

In 1750 North Carolina's population had increased to fifty thousand. In 1753 on the eve of the French and Indian War its population was eighty thousand. At the end of the war it had climbed to one hundred and twenty thousand, as colonists sought safety from the Indians. By the outbreak of the Revolutionary War in 1775, North Carolina had two hundred sixty-five thousand whites and eighty thousand blacks, becoming the fourth largest colony in the empire behind Virginia, Pennsylvania, and Massachusetts.

In 1729 seven of the eight proprietors sold their rights to the crown, and North Carolina became a royal colony. Lord Granville, John Carteret, retained his share.

The first town in North Carolina was Edenton on Albemarle Sound. New Bern was next, and Wilmington with its deep-water harbor, was third.

The Quakers also had a meeting at New Garden. In 1754 forty-five families from Pennsylvania, one from Maryland, thirty-five from Virginia, and four from New England formed it. In the early 1770s forty-one families from Nantucket Island, Massachusetts, joined them. They included the Starbucks and Swaims. The Piedmont of North Carolina lacked a dependency on slave labor, so the Quakers were comfortable in locating there.

Scottish Highlanders settled in the southern part of the colony on the Cape River. They began arriving in 1732 and disembarked at Brunswick or Wilmington. James Innes had a grant of 320 acres in 1732 and another of 640 acres in 1733. Hugh Campbell had a grant of 640 acres in the same year as did William Forbes. They were the vanguard. In 1739 a ship load of Highland Scots from Argyleshire under the guidance of Neil McNeill of Kintyre, Scotland, arrived. Over three hundred fifty ships came; more of them came to North Carolina than to any other colony. They were the only large group of colonists to come to North Carolina directly. Three hundred and fifty arrived in 1739 from Argyleshire and settled in the Cross Creek area. Gabriel Johnston became royal governor in 1732. He was a Scot and was responsible for the beginning of large scale settlement of his countrymen. The legislature in 1740 recognized them as "foreign Protestants" and released them from taxes for their first ten years in the colony. Led by Neil McNeil, they landed at Wilmington in 1740. Their settlement was included in Cumberland County when it was created in 1754.

Duane Meyer's *The Highland Scots of North Carolina 1732-1776* (Raleigh, State Dept. of Archives & History, 1968) is not to be confused with Scots Irish. The large settlement in Fayette County is the focus of Scott Buie's *North Carolina Scottish Ancestry* (Fort Worth, Tex.: the author, 1991).

In the early eighteenth century, Arthur Dobbs and Henry McCulloh sought to bring a hundred twenty poor Protestant families from Ireland to the head of the northeast Cape Fear River. They settled in Duplin County.

Christopher von Graffenriedt sought to introduce Palatines to North Carolina. Some 650 Palatines set sail from London in January 1710. Half of them died on the thirteen-week trans-Atlantic crossing. They landed at Virginia on James river. One of their vessels was plundered by a French privateer. By autumn Von Graffenreidt reached his destination at Bern, North Carolina.

A year later the Indians massacred most of the colonists. Five hundred Tuscarora warriors struck and killed between a hundred thirty and one hundred and forty colonists. They took twenty to thirty prisoners. In the summer and fall of 1712 the Indians launched another attack. They lost nine hundred and fifty of their number. The removal of the Indian threat opened up the area to settlement.

Between 1747 and 1750, Pennsylvania Germans began moving to North Carolina via the Upper Road east of the Shenandoah valley. From Philadelphia via Lancaster and York they traveled through Monocacy, Maryland and Fredericktown to Leesburg, across piedmont Virginia to Hillsborough, North Carolina, and then to Bethabara. Joseph and Jacob Shook received land in 1749 in Burke County. In 1753 the Moravians set up Wachovia. Bishop Spangenberg had visited the area and selected the site in Forsyth County on a 98,985 acre tract that they had purchased from Lord Granville. The first group of Moravians to arrive were fifteen unmarried men. The Moravian bachelors went to Old Broadbay and Waldoboro, Maine, for wives. Bethabara and Bethania were their next settlements as more Brethren joined them. They came from Bethlehem and Nazareth, Pennsylvania. During the French and Indian War, the Carolina Indians attacked the Moravian settlement. The settlers fled to safety at Salem. By 1766 Bethabara had one hundred thirty inhabitants and the latter eighty-seven; Levin T. Reichel's *The Moravians in North Carolina* (Baltimore: Genealogical Publishing Co., 1968) describes the sect and their history. Salem was a flourishing village of a hundred twenty people in 1772. The success of the Moravian settlers encouraged other Germans to locate in North Carolina.

When Rowan County was created in 1753, the County seat of Salisbury was thirty miles south of Wachovia. By 1762 it boasted sixteen public houses to accommodate travelers and was becoming an important trading center. It was chartered as a town in 1768. While there had been no Germans west of the Yadkin in 1746 and only a few in 1752, they were there in significant numbers by 1762.

The colonial Germans soon became camouflaged. Johannes Eckel became John Eagel and Franz Oberkirsch became Francis Overcash. Members of a Klein family appeared as Peter Klein, John Kline, Jacob Cline, John Small, George Little, and William Short. Zimmermans became Carpenters and Schneiders became Taylors.

Gotthardt D. Bernheim's, *History of the German Settlements and of the Lutheran Church in North and South Carolina from the Earliest Period of the Colonization of the Dutch, German, and Swiss Settlers to the Close of the First Half of the Present Century* (Spartanburg, S. C.: Reprint Co., 1972), Johnny Elwood Reasonover's *First Palatines in North Carolina* (Lubbock, Texas, the author, 1979), and John Henry Clewell's, *History* of *Wachovia in North Carolina* .... (Doubleday, Page & Co., 1902) treat the German colonists in the Tar Heel State.

When the Bloody Duke of Cumberland defeated the Highland Scots at Culloden in 1746, the Scots suffered the breakup of their clan system. They were forbidden to bear arms or to wear their traditional dress–the kilt. Their estates were confiscated. King George II offered all Scots who would take an oath of allegiance and immigrate to America a pardon. Thousands did so.

Between 1769 and 1772, there were sixteen hundred Scots from Argyll and Aarran who arrived in North Carolina. Their number had climbed to twelve thousand by the time of the American Revolution.

In the 1730s, Pennsylvania and Delaware Welsh settlers came to New Hanover and Sampson counties on the west bank of the Cape Fear river. Some others may have come from South Carolina.

Also in the 1730s, poor Protestants from Ireland settled near the head of the Cape Fear River on Black river in Duplin County. By 1740 Ulster Scots had migrated via the valley of Virginia to North Carolina where they populated Rowan, Orange, Mecklenburg, Guilford, Davidson, and Cabarrus counties. In 1745 Governor Arthur Dobbs, a native of Ulster, had a grant of 4,000 acres in Mecklenburg and Cabarrus counties and another tract in New Hanover County with colonists recruited from Carrickfergus and County Antrim. He had to have one white settler for every 200 acres. By 1755 there were seventy-eight families on his grant, but only eighteen were from Ireland.

The Scots-Irish fled to North Carolina from Virginia during the French and Indian War. They were dissenters and were eager to escape the taxes of the established Church.

Shubal Stearns, who was born in Boston in 1706, became a Baptist at Tolland, Connecticut, in 1751. With a few other Baptists, he removed to Opeckon, Berkeley County, Virginia. Some of his friends in Randolph County, North Carolina, begged him to come and preach to them. The eight families who constituted the congregation contained many of his relatives. They included Peter Stearns, Ebenezer Stearns, Daniel Marshall, Joseph Breed, Enos Stimpson, and Jonathan Polk.

The Regulator War pitted the Piedmont residents against the Tidewater power brokers in a struggle from 1768 to 1771. The Regulators petitioned the royal governor for redress in 1768, but Governor Tryon repulsed them. The Regulators in turn turned out a force of three thousand seven hundred men when some of the leaders were to be tried in the Hillsborough District Court. Governor Tyron called out one thousand four hundred sixty-one militiamen to protect the court, and the rebels withdrew. Armed bands attacked the jails where their leaders were incarcerated. They assaulted local courts and interrupted proceedings. They treated governmental officials with contempt and bodily injury.

In 1771 the forces of Governor Tryon squashed the Regulators in the battle of Alamance on the 6th of May. Many of the participants took refuge in the western part of North Carolina and eastern Tennessee.

South Carolina

The colony of South Carolina began with the sailing of three ships from England in August 1669. The first stop was Kinsale, Ireland, where the captain hoped to take on board more colonists. Instead, some of the passengers opted to jump ship. It was another forty days to Barbados, where the colonists remained for four months before the last leg of their journey. They replenished their supplies and purchased livestock. A number of Barbadians joined them. A family from Nevis also joined them. One of the ships was lost in a tropical storm; it was replaced by a thirty-ton sloop built in Barbados. In 1670 the three vessels set sail for South Carolina. The eastern storms caused one of the ships to run aground in the Bahamas. The last two ships headed for Bermuda. Only one ship with the majority of the colonists numbering one hundred thirty, reached South Carolina. During the next two years about half of the white colonists were from Barbados. Between 1670 and 1690 about 54 percent of the whites came from the British West Indies. These included the Beadon, Colleton, Daniel, Drayton, Fenwicke, Gibbes, Godfrey, Ladson, Middleton, Moore, Schenckingh, and Yeamans from Barbados. From Jamaica came the Amory, Parris, Pinckney, and Whaley families. From St. Christopher's came the Lowndes and Rawlins. The LaMottes came from Grenada and the Woodwards from Nevis.

Agnes Baldwin's *First Settlers of South Carolina 1670-80* (Columbia: University of South Carolina Press, 1969) contains every reference to anyone in the colony in its first decade.

Charles Town was initially laid out 25 miles from the mouth of the Ashley River which was surrounded by water on three sides. The settlement could not be seen from the harbor, so the feared Spanish could not see the English. Within a decade the town was relocated at the junction of the Ashley and Cooper rivers. Since tobacco did not do well in the swampy colony and since English grains were ill-suited to the semi-tropical environment, Charles Town did not come into its own until the 1690s when the colonists began to experiment with rice culture imported from the islands.

The Spanish were at St. Augustine, Florida, 250 miles down the coast, and the English at Jamestown 400 miles to the north. South Carolina turned to the fur trade for its economic basis. The English allied themselves with Indian tribes who had not been befriended by the Spanish. By the 1690s, the colony was shipping fifty-four thousand deer skins to London annually.

Stuart's Town was established in 1682 as a Scottish colony. The settlers had sailed from Gourock Bay on the Clyde. Among them were the Hamiltons, Montgomerys, and Dunlops. Four years later the Spanish attacked and destroyed it. Some of the survivors fled to Charleston and others migrated north to Virginia.

In December 1695 a group of Puritans from Dorchester, Massachusetts Bay, moved to South Carolina, where they founded the town of Dorchester twenty miles up the Ashley River. From Concord came Joshua Brooks, Nathaniel Billings, and Simon Daken. William Adams was from Sudbury. Increase Sumner and William Pratt were from Dorchester, and George Fox was from Reading. They sailed from Boston on the *Friendship*. The voyage took fifteen days. In 1696 the Sumners, Kelleys, Chamberlains, Osgoods, Pratts, Normans, and Ways joined the settlement. The soil was poor and sandy, so they decided to relocate as a congregation to Medway, Georgia.

Another New England migration involved The Rev. William Screven, who probably came from Somersetshire, England, to Kittery, Maine. He became active among the Baptists, which brought him into disfavor with the Puritan establishment. He refused to pay the fine levied upon him and was imprisoned. In 1682 he was licensed to preach by the Baptists in Boston. He was ordered to leave Maine, but he managed to linger and organized a Baptist church at Kittery.

South Carolina offered religious toleration. Screven's wife, Bridget Cutt, had come to South Carolina from Barbados, and a number of settlers in South Carolina also came from Somersetshire. In 1696 Screven received a warrant for 1,000 acres of land and another for 1,500 acres. Neighboring grantees included Permanus Screven, Elizabeth and Robert Wetherick, Champernoun Elliott, and Humphrey Axtell. They formed the nucleus of settlers from Maine.

In 1703 South Carolina had a population of more than 7,000. Almost half were black slaves. The free whites numbered 3,600, of whom the majority were from Barbados.

South Carolina had the largest French population of the British colonies per capita. More than ten thousand came. Forty-five Huguenots arrived in 1680. Most of them settled north and east along the Cooper River and on the Santee River. Their parishes were St. Thomas and St. Denis.

48

Among the Huguenot families were the Bonneau, Cordes, DeSaussure, Deveaux, DuBose, Fort, Gaillard, Gendron, Guerard, Horry, Huger, Laurens, Legare, Manigualt, Marion, Peyre, Procher, Prioleau, Ravenel, Simons, and Timothy.

Settling in St. John's Berkeley were the Huguenot families of Mayzkes, Ravenels, St. Juliens, Guignards, Laurens, Hugers, Porchers, and Le Nobles. Harry A. Davis's *Some Huguenot Families of South Carolina and Georgia* (Washington, D. C. 1927 and Supplement 1937), Arthur H. Hirsch's *The Huguenots of Colonial South Carolina* (Baltimore: Genealogical Publishing Co., 2009), and Daniel Ravenel's *Liste des francois et suisses* (Baltimore: Genealogical Publishing Co., 1968) cover the Huguenots as does R. M. Golden's *The Huguenot Connection: The Edict of Nantes, Its Revocation, and Early French Migration to South Carolina* (Washington, D.C., 1927). Vast coverage appears in the *Transactions of the Huguenot Society of South Carolina*, v. I (1889) and its cumulative index 1889-1994. Bertrand Van Rumbeke's *From New Babylon to Eden: The Huguenots and Their Migration to Colonial South Carolina* (Columbia, S, C.: University of South Carolina Press, 2006) expands the older literature.

During the French and Indian War, 1754 to 1763, England expelled the French inhabitants from Nova Scotia and settled them in other English colonies. Two thousand Acadians were deported to Massachusetts, 700 to Connecticut, 250 to New York, 500 to Pennsylvania, 1,000 to Maryland, 1,100 to Virginia, 500 to North Carolina, 500 to South Carolina, and 400 to Georgia in 1755. They were Roman Catholics in Protestant English territory. In 1756 those sent to Virginia were rerouted to England. In 1758 the 2,500 who avoided being deported by escaping to Louisburg were deported to England and France. At the end of the war, many left the English colonies and emigrated to Quebec and the Maritimes as well as San Dominque, Guadeloupe, and Martinque. Those in the Carolinas, Georgia, and Maryland relocated in Louisiana and Haiti. In 1764 the Acadians in Virginia who had been sent to England were sent to France. They returned to North America and settled in Louisiana. Another two hundred left Halifax, Nova Scotia, for Louisiana in 1766.

In the 1720s South Carolina began wooing the Indian tribes. The Alabama and Yamasee, however, remained loyal to the French. The British also won over the Yazoo and Natchez tribes with their superior English goods.

In 1729 South Carolina ceased to be a proprietary colony and became a royal colony.

In 1730 the Board of Trade directed Gov. Robert Johnson to survey eleven townships on the frontier of South Carolina to protect the coastal settlements from both the Spaniards and the Indians. The townships were to be located 60 miles inland on the colony's principal rivers from the Waccamaw River in the north to the Altamaha River in the south. Each township was to contain 20,000 acres and measure 6 miles on each side. Each person who settled in these townships was to receive 50 acres for each member of the household. The colony would provide funds for tools, transportation, and food. Quit rents were to be waived for ten years. In 1755 the head of a family was to receive 100 acres and every other member of his household 50 acres per person. There were nine townships and one semi-township established by 1759. Three more were established before the Revolutionary War. They were Purrysburg and New Windsor on the Savannah River, Saxe Gotha on the Congaree, Orangeburg on the Edisto, Amelia near the juncture of the Congaree with the Santee, Williamsburg on the Black River, Queensborough on the Great Pee Dee, and Kingston on the Waccamaw. The semi-township was the Welsh Tract laid out adjacent to Queensborough.

In November 1735 about two dozen people from the Welsh Tract Baptist Church in Delaware were dismissed to the Baptist Church in Charleston. The next year a group petitioned for 10,000 acres in Queensborough Township, eight miles on either side of the Pee Dee River for 70 miles. The Welsh Tract had three Baptist churches. By 1760 there were 3,200 settlers and 300 slaves on the Welsh Tract. Welsh families included Griffith, David, Gillespie, Ellerbe, Rowland, Lewis, and Jones.

By the 1760s Boonesborough on Long Cane Creek, Hillsborough at the confluence of Little river and Long Cane creek, and Londonborough on Hard Labor creek had been settled. The latter was established in 1762 for Irish immigrants.

Purysburg and Hillsborough were French settlements. Jean Pierre Pury was a French Swiss whose first contingent of sixty-one residents arrived. The Switzers numbered 800 by the 1740s. Hillsborough was laid out in 1764. The Rev. Jean Louis Guibert brought French Huguenots to his settlement. They built two small towns named for their homes in France: New Bordeaux and New Rochelle. Susan Baldwin Bates and Harriott Cheves Leland's *French Santee, A Huguenot Settlement in Colonial South Carolina* (Baltimore: Otter Bay Books, 2015) is an exhaustive study.

South Carolina introduced the Bounty Act of 1761 in order to reduce the ratio of free settlers to slaves. The act authorized £4 sterling. The payment went to the one who imported the colonist. Each colonist also received 20 shillings for necessities. The act was allowed to lapse in 1768. Between three and four thousand immigrants arrived in the colony under the scheme. About one-fourth of them were Germans.

Other Germans had come to South Carolina in the 1730s, lured by the promise of a 50 acre headright. They lacked the funds to pay their passage and had to sell themselves or their children into indentured servitude for a period of years. They came as families. These Germans settled in Orangeburg and Amelia townships. In the 1740s more Germans arrived and settled in Saxe Gotha Township. More Germans arrived in the 1750s.

Three hundred Palatine Germans came to Charleston. Forty-five died on the trans-Atlantic crossing, and many of the arrivals were ill. Those who survived settled in Londonborough Township on Hard Labor creek. In nearby New Windsor Township half of the settlers were also Germans. Most of the Germans were Lutherans, but some of them became members of the Church of England. The Rev. John Gissendanner provided them with a German edition of the *Book of Common Prayer*. Amaker, Boozer, Geiger, Harmon, Inabinet, Kalteisen, Lever, Lorick, Rast, Sheeley, Shuler, Theur, Wannamaker, and Zeigler were some of the surnames of the colonists.

The first Jews arrived in Charleston in 1749. Barret A. Elzas, *The Jews of South Carolina from the Earliest Times to the Present Day* (Spartanburg: Reprint Company, 1972) covers the migration. In the 1750s, settlers arrived via the Great Wagon Road. Settlers arrived in North America at the port of Philadelphia, moved westward to Harrisburg, Pennsylvania, and traveled via the Shenandoah Valley of Virginia to the Piedmont. The Scots Irish and Pennsylvania Dutch from Pennsylvania, Maryland, and Virginia were the most numerous. They settled in the Waxhaws and along Long Cane Creek and made their way into the wilderness along the buffalo paths. Common among their surnames were the Adair, Bratton, Caldwell, Calhoun, Logan, Montgomery, Moore, Ross, and Wardlaw.

Other Scots-Irish came directly to South Carolina from Ireland. The Rev. William Martin led his congregation in 1722. There were four hundred sixty-seven families in the group migration. One of his congregants was a Mr. Beck. His landlord's rent collector called upon Beck to pay up or be evicted. Mrs. Beck was giving birth to a child, and Mr. Beck resisted by throwing the landlord's agent out the door. In the melee the agent's neck was broken. Both the wife and child died, and Beck disappeared. The Rev. Martin foretold that the same would befall the rest of his congregation. Five ship loads opted to come to South Carolina.

The Scots-Irish, along with the Germans and English, were lured to South Carolina by a generous colonial land policy of one hundred acres to the head of a family and fifty acres for each additional household member. The port of Charleston was a major one for the export of crops, and the colonists could settle anywhere they chose.

Settlers in South Carolina in the post French and Indian war period included Levi P. Doughty, who was born in Chatham County, North Carolina, where he lived before settling in Darlington District. He later moved west to East Feliciana Parish, Louisiana where he died in 1854 at the age of 91 years. His great-great grandfather was Edward Doty of the *Mayflower*. He was the first Pilgrim descendant to live in the Pelican State.

Dr. Jean Stephenson's *Scotch-Irish Migrations to South Carolina 1770* (Vienna, Virginia.: the author, 1971) names four thousand colonists who traveled on five ships led by The Rev. William Martin.

Janie Revill's *A Compilation of the Original Lists of Protestant Immigrants to South Carolina* (Baltimore: Genealogical Publishing Co., 1981) covers the period from the French and Indian War to the Revolutionary War.

At the time of the Revolutionary War, South Carolina was the wealthiest colony in British North America. In the low country there were 104,000 blacks and 70,000 whites. The back country had 46,000 whites.

With the various Indian cessions and removals in the South in the aftermath of the Revolutionary War, nine out of every twenty South Carolinians went west or to the old Southwest. From Columbia, South Carolina, to Augusta, Milledgeville, Macon, and Columbus, Georgia, they made their way to Montgomery, Selma, and St. Stephens, Alabama to Natchez, Mississippi, Natchitoches, Louisiana, and Nacogdoches, Texas.

Georgia
Georgia is the largest state in square miles in the eastern half of the nation, so it was the last to be occupied with any significant population.

Georgia was the only colony to be planted under the Hanoverian monarchs. The colony was in a precarious position between the English and the Spanish. Twenty-five families arrived in 1733. A small group of forty Jews came in the summer of 1733. They included the Sheftal, DeLyon, Minis, and Nun families. James Oglethorpe and the Trustees had difficulty in convincing Englishmen to risk settling in Georgia, causing the colony's officials to turn elsewhere for settlers. In March 1734 they invited the Salzburgers. They were Protestants, mostly Lutherans, who resided in the principality of Salzburg ruled by a Roman Catholic Archbishop who persecuted them. They arrived in Georgia in 1736 and founded Ebenezer on the Savannah river in Effingham County. John Martin Bolzius led the band of seventy-eight colonists. A second contingent arrived in 1736. By 1741 there were twelve thousand Salzburgers in Georgia. In King George's War, when the Spanish attacked the colony in 1735, the pacifistic Salzburgers were called upon to defend the colony. Rather than compromise their faith, many of them relocated in Pennsylvania where they could practice their religion according to their own dictates. Other settled in North Carolina.

Adelaide L. Fries' *The Moravians in Georgia, 1735-1740* (Baltimore: Genealogical Publishing Co., 1967), Philip S. Strobel's *The Salzburgers and Their Descendants* (Baltimore: Genealogical Publishing Co., 1967), Pearl (Rahn) Gann's *Georgia Salzburgers and Allied Families* (Easley, S.C. Southern Historical Press, 1979), Samuel Urlssperger, *Detailed Reports on the Salzburger Emigrants Who Settled in America 1733-1736* (Easley, S.C. Southern Historical Press, 1980), and George F. Jones, *The Salzburger Saga; Religious Exiles and Other Germans along the Savannah* (Atlanta: University of Georgia Press, 1984) treat these German-speaking colonists.

Moravians arrived in 1735. A second band of Salzburgers and Moravians arrived in 1736.

Oglethorpe then sought Scottish Highlanders to colonize his lands. The Mackintoshes, Baileys, Dunbars, Mackays, and Cuthberts came from Inverness, Scotland to settle the southern outposts of his colony. They arrived in January 1736. They called their settlement New Inverness. Later it became known as Darien. The Rev. John McLeod led the hundred and thirty settlers to Georgia. They were soldiers and farmers and came with their families in return for free land and provisions for a year. David Dobson's *Scots in Georgia and the Deep South* (Baltimore: Genealogical Publishing Co., 2000) treats the Scots. Five miles from Savannah was Highgate, where French Huguenots settled. Germans and Swiss settled at Vernonburg.

There was a settlement of New England Puritans at Dorchester, South Carolina, which was located in an unhealthy environment and in need of more vacant land for expansion. Georgia offered them 22,400 acres, and in 1752 and 1753 more than eight hundred removed to Georgia. Among them were the Andrews, Bacon, Baker, Burnley, Elliott, Mitchell, Osgood, Quarterman, Spencer, Stevens, Sumner, and Way households. In 1755 they were joined by the Girardeau, Gortons, Luptons, and Winns.

Quakers came into the colony in 1760 and settled at Wrightsboro in McDuffie County.

The trusteeship expired in 1753, and Georgia became a royal colony.

The state of Georgia had a bounty land program for Revolutionary War veterans or noncombatants or their heirs. The land lay in the southern portion of Franklin County and the northern part of Washington County between the Oconee and Appalachee rivers.

In 1793 Eli Whitney invented his cotton gin. Before that time the long staple cotton of the sea islands of Georgia and South Carolina was the only variety that could be used. The seeds could be removed by hand from the cotton. Whitney's gin made it possible to do the same with short staple green cotton and inaugurated the agricultural revolution of the next century. Georgia held six land lotteries for entrants who met the residency requirements. They were held in 1805, 1807, 1820, 1821, 1827, and 1832. Virginia S. and R.V. Wood's *The 1805 Land Lottery of Georgia* (Easley, South Carolina: Southern Historical Press, 1864) has 25,000 winners; Silas E, Lucas, *The 1807 Land Lottery of Georgia* (Easley, South Carolina: Southern Historical Press, 1968) has 12,000 winners; *The 1820 Land Lottery of Georgia* (Easley, South Carolina: Southern Historical Press, 1977) lists more than 25,000 winners; *The 1821 Land Lottery of Georgia* (Easley, South Carolina: Southern Historical Press, 1971) identifies 17,000 winners; Martha Houston's *The 1827 Land Lottery of Georgia* (Easley, South Carolina, Southern Historical Press, 1967) has 15,000 winners; and Silas E. Lucas's *The 1832 Gold Lottery of Georgia* (Easley, South Carolina: Southern Historical Press, 1981) lists 20,000 winners. The 1805 lottery was the only one to list the losers.

In 1828 America's second gold rush was at Dahlonega, Georgia. Thousands of miners came to make their fortunes. The location was on the lands of the Cherokee Indian Nation and brought about the seizure of their lands.

Tecumseh, a Shawnee chieftain, proposed an Indian state be created and admitted to the Union on the same basis as other states. The United States sought to displace the Cherokees, Creeks, Chickasaws, Choctaws, and Seminoles to reservation lands west of the Mississippi River. John Ross led the Cherokee in Georgia, North Carolina, South Carolina, and Tennessee in contesting the forced removal. John Ross's father was a Scottish immigrant and his mother was one-eighth Cherokee. By 1838 only two thousand had obeyed the edict of removal. The journey was known as the Trail of Tears. Six months later the Cherokee arrived in Oklahoma in March 1839.

The governor of Georgia issued passports to citizens relocating to the Louisiana and Mississippi territories between 1785 and 1809. Dorothy Williams Potter's, *Passports of Southeastern Pioneers, 1770-1823 Indian, Spanish, and Other Land Passports for Tennessee, Kentucky, Georgia, Mississippi, Virginia, North and South Carolina* (Baltimore: Genealogical Publishing Co., 1982) makes available this little known source.

Chapter Six: The Impact of the Revolutionary War

At the outbreak of the Revolutionary War, Britain had fifteen thousand troops in North America. There were 3,000,000 people in the colonies. Britain lacked sufficient troops to meet the emergency. Britain was a nation dependent on her seamen for defense and to guard against a second regicide by disgruntled citizens. Following the battle of Bunker Hill, the British approached Catherine the Great of Russia and asked to hire twenty thousand troops. She declined their offer, so the British next approached the Dutch, who also declined. Since King George III was also the Elector of Hanover, he decided to use his Hanoverian troops to man outposts elsewhere in the empire and thereby free soldiers for service in America. Gibraltar was one such case.

The English relied on their naval power for defense. Because of the fate of the late King Charles, the English preferred to keep their military forces at sea rather than on land. King George authorized Lt. Col. Albrecht Scheither to recruit two thousand men in Hanover. Scheither signed up only two hundred fifty. He recruited another one thousand eight hundred sixty-eight men along the Rhine River and Bavaria but one hundred sixty-one were found to be unfit for military service. Therefore, the British monarch turned to his former allies from the French and Indian War. Clifford N. Smith's *British and German Deserters, Dischargees, and Prisoners of War Who May Have Remained in Canada and the United States 1774-1783 and Muster Rolls and Prisoner-of-War Lists in American Archival Collections Pertaining to the German Mercenary Troops Who Served with British Forces during the American Revolution. Deserters and Disbanded Soldiers from British, German, Loyalists Military Units in the South, 1782* (Baltimore: Clearfield, 2004) and Heinrich Armin, *Some German-American Participants in the American Revolution: the Ratterman Lists* (McNeal, Arizona, Westland Publications, 1990) untangle and expand the data.

The terms mercenaries and auxiliaries have become used incorrectly. A mercenary is a private soldier who enlists in a foreign government army. The Marquis de Lafayette would be such an example. He was a French subject who entered the American army. Auxiliary troops are those hired by another foreign government. The Americans were waging a war and sought public opinion by falsely portraying the Germans as mercenaries rather than as auxiliary troops.

Six German monarchs furnished about thirty thousand troops. The German troops represented a third of the British army in North America. More auxiliary troops came from Hesse which accounts for all German troops being called Hessians. The agreements made with some of these monarchs included a blood money clause that if a soldier failed to return his monarch would receive double compensation. Many of these monarchs enrolled troops who were born in other German states.

Duke Carl of Braunschweig Wolfenbutel agreed to furnish 3,964 infantrymen and 336 cavalry. Clifford N. Smith, *Brunswick Deserter Immigrants of the American Revolution* (Thomson, Illinois: Heritage House, 1973). The British agreed to pay a bounty for each man and subsidy for each soldier for two years after the war.

The Landgrave of Hesse-Kassel, whose wife was an aunt of King George, furnished about fifteen thousand men in four grenadier battalions, one courier corps, and one military corps, according to Kurt Dulfer, *Hessische Truppen im Amerikanischen Unabhae nggikeitskrieg* (Marburg: Archivschule, 1972). Hessen-Hanau furnished two thousand four hundred and twenty-two, of which nine hundred eighty-one never returned to Germany. Clifford Neal Smith's, *Mercenaries from Hessen-Hanau Who Remained in Canada and the United States after the American Revolution* (DeKalb, Illinois: Westland Publications, 1976) covers this German state. Many of the soldiers brought their wives and families or acquired same in America. [See Clifford N. Smith's *Annotated Hessian Chaplaincy Records of the American Revolution, 1776-1784: Christenings, Marriages, and Deaths* (McNeal, Arizona: Westland Publications, 1994)]. Smith's *Notes on Hessian Soldiers Who Remained in Canada and the United States after the American Revolution. 1775-1784* (McNeal, Arizona: Westland Publication, 1994), Braunschweig sent 5,723 soldiers, of which 2,708 returned to Europe. Many of them were taken prisoner at Saratoga in 1778 and held in captivity. In January 1779 they were marched to Charlottesville, Virginia. The Virginians did not have the means to maintain them and allowed them to fend for themselves. After the war may of them migrated into Kentucky and Tennessee. Many also returned to their units and opted for bounty land in Canada described in Clifford N. Smith's *Brunswick Deserter Immigrants of the American Revolution* (Thomson, Ill.: Heritage House, 1973). Anhalt Zerbst's troops served in New York and Canada. *Vide* Clifford N. Smith, *Mercenary Troops from Anhalt-Zerbst, Germany Who Remained in America after the Revolution* (Thomson, Ill., Heritage House, 1974).

Ansbach Bayreuth sent 2,353 soldiers to America; 1,183 returned to Europe. Many of them were captured and interned at Lancaster and Reading, Pennsylvania. A significant number returned to their units and were given land in Canada. Ninety-five married and remained in Canada. *Vide* Clifford N. Smith, *Mercenaries from Ansbach and Bayreuth, Germans Who Remained in America after the American Revolution* and Erhard Staedtler, *Die Ansbach-Bayreuther Truppen im Amerikanischen Unabhaenggkeiskrieg* (Nurnberg,(n. p., 1955).

Of the 19,000 from Hessen-Kassel 3,000 stayed in America, of whom 2,500 settled in Canada in Clements Township, Annapolis County, Nova Scotia.

The contracts with Braunschweig, Hessen-Hanau, and Waldeck stipulated that for soldiers who died or were killed in North America, the British were to pay $35 rather than the $11.66. This blood money clause was in effect a double indemnity feature. It was to the advantage of the German monarchs whose contracts contained the double indemnity clause to pad their accounts with casualties when, in fact, the soldiers were deserters.

There were 1,225 men from Waldeck, of whom 470 were natives of the principality. Five hundred returned to Europe leaving 250 in North America. Bruce E. Burgoyne's *The Waldeck Soldiers of the American Revolution.* (Bowie, Md.; Heritage Books, 1991) names the 1,225.

Lion G. Miles' *Hessians of Lewis Miller*, (Lyndhurst, Ohio: Johannes Schwalm Historical Association, 1983) is a work of portraiture of Hessian prisoners-of-war in Pennsylvania.

Of the 39,667 auxiliary troops 17,313 returned to Europe leaving unaccounted 12,554. These soldier immigrants constituted the largest single wave of Germans to come to the United States in the 18th century.

Many colonists remained loyal to the crown. Americans referred to them as the Tories. After the war more than 5,800 loyalists filed claims for compensation. Some three-quarters left the United States but about 1,400 remained behind. There were instances of those who deserted their German units and joined British units. Christopher George Dillman deserted his Hessian unit in May 1776 and joined the 8th Regiment in New York. At the end of the war he was discharged and settled in Nova Scotia.

The Journal of the Johannes Schwalm Historical Association, 1981-2004 began to identify auxiliary troopers who remained in America and established families.

The Revolutionary War was also a civil war. Those who fought for the Crown and remained supporters of the empire were known as Loyalists. They were more likely to be from urban centers such as Savannah, Georgia; Charleston, South Carolina; Boston, Massachusetts; Norfolk, Virginia; Annapolis and Baltimore, Maryland, and New York City, New York. New York Loyalists accounted for half of those raised as soldiers in the war. New York expelled more Loyalists than any other colony. New York confiscated their property and used it to retire their war debt. New York realized $3,600,000.

Murtie June Clark's *Loyalists in the Southern Campaign of the Revolutionary War* (Baltimore: Genealogical Publishing Co., 3 vols. 1980-81) lists 35,000 Loyalists. Her first volume contains those recruited from North Carolina, South Carolina, Georgia, Mississippi and Florida, Volume II has Louisiana. Maryland, Pennsylvania, and Virginia; and Volume III has New Jersey and New York. Other Loyalist sources include Clifford S. Dwyer, *Index to Series I of American Loyalists Claims* and *Index to Series II of American Loyalists Claims (Athens.*: Iberian, 1990). Peter Wilson Coldham's *American Migrations, 1765-1799* (Washington, D.C.: National Genealogical Society, 1980) Paul J. Bunnell *'s The New Loyalist Index 3* vols. (Bowie, Md.:Heritage Books, 1989) has many Loyalists from Cape Cod, the islands of Nantucket, and Martha's Vineyard.

Georgia, New York, and South Carolina contributed the largest percentage of their population to the Loyalists, who were also disproportionally represented among governmental officials, merchants, Anglicans, Scots and Ulstermen, Indians, recent arrivals, veterans of the French and Indian War who had bounty lands in southern New York and the back country of the Carolinas, and recent arrivals from the Mother Country. More than twenty-five thousand served. In 1780 to 1782 there were three 312 companies of Provincial Corps consisting of ten thousand soldiers. Those who went to East and West Florida felt betrayed when England was forced to cede these colonies to her opponent the Spain after the war. That caused the American Loyalists one more removal .Wilbur Henry Siebert treated the Loyalists in East and West Florida in *Loyalist in East Florida. 1774-1785: the Most Important Documents Pertaining Thereto* and "The Loyalists in West Florida and the Natchez District," *Mississippi Valley Historical Review,* II (1916) 465-83.

Some Canadians joined in the struggle for independence. Virginia E. DeMarce, *Canadian Participants in the American Revolution* (Arlington, Virginia.: the author, 1980.) W. Bruce Antliff, *Loyalist Settlements 1783-1789* (Ontario, 1983, *The Centennial of the Settlement of Upper Canada by the United Empire Loyalists* (Boston: Gregg Press, 1972), Linda Croupe, *Index to the Loyalists of the Eastern Townships of Quebec* (the author, no date), and Virginia DeMarce's *Canadian Regiments in the American Revolution* (the author, 1980) reveal the conflict as a civil war. Stewart E. Dunaway's *North Carolina Land Confiscation Records* (Morrison, the author, 2010, 3 vols.) fills the paper trail of land records.

Chapter Seven: Post-Revolutionary War Settlements

With the defeat of the British at Yorktown and the Treaty of Paris in 1783, many British subjects opted to leave the United States of America. The British colony of Nova Scotia received thirty-five thousand refugees. Quebec received ten thousand. Twelve thousand went to East and West Florida, two thousand to the Bahamas, three thousand to Jamaica, and five thousand went to England. Loyalists from the middle colonies removed to that part of Quebec that became Ontario. They made claims for confiscated properties, giving their former places of residence and nativity. These are in Alexander Fraser's *United Empire Loyalists: Enquiry into the Losses and Services in Consequence of Their Loyalty in Evidence in the Canadian Claims* in the two-volume *Second Report of the Bureau of Archives for the Province of Ontario* (Baltimore: Genealogical Publishing Co., 1994).

Loyalist American blacks established Freetown in Sierra Leone in Africa.

Loyalist members of the same family might have had various destinations. Louisa Wells from Charleston, South Carolina, went to England as did her parents. Her two brothers, William and James, went to East Florida, and her fiancee went to Jamaica.

By 1791 the Americans had cleared more land than the French had cleared in New France. They were well adapted to forest colonization, and their success accounted for their expansion.

In 1783 there were 45,000 Americans living in western Pennsylvania; 15,000 were in north central Kentucky, 10,000 were in eastern Tennessee at Watauga, and another 3,000 were in central Tennessee on the Cumberland River. There were 30,000 Indians in the Old Northwest. They were the Shawnee, Wyandot, Delaware, Mingo, Ottawa, Chippewa, Miami, and Potawatomi. In the Old Southwest the Cherokee, Creek, Choctaw, and Chickasaw numbered 50,000.

The western border of the newly established nation was the Mississippi River, and the new nation had a tremendous war debt to pay off. The largest asset of the new country was the western land, and it became the major force of drawing settlers westward. There were two routes available. The northern route was via the Ohio River valley. Settlers could follow the Pennsylvania Road and Forbes's Road to Pittsburgh and descend the Ohio River in flat boats. River traffic was inaugurated between Pittsburgh and Cincinnati in 1794. An advertisement in the press announced that:

"Two boats will travel Cincinnati and Pittsburgh. The first boat leaves Cincinnati at 8 o'clock and returns to Cincinnati so as to sail again in four weeks. The proprietors of these boats having naturally considered the many inconveniences and dangers incident to the common method heretofore adopted of navigating the Ohio and being influenced by the love of philanthropy, and desirous of being serviceable to the public, has taken great pains to render the accommodations on board as agreeable and convenient as they can profitably be made. No danger need be apprehended from the enemy (Indians) as every person on board will be under cover, made proof against rifle or musket ball; convenient port-holes for firing will be found on each boat."

The southern route was overland through the Cumberland Gap. Between 1783 and 1800, nearly three hundred thousand settlers passed through the Gap to settle in Kentucky, Tennessee, and Ohio. In 1788 and 1789, between eight and nine hundred flat boats went down the Ohio to Fort

Harmar. They transported 20,000 people, 7,000 horses, 30,000 cows, 900 sheep, and 600 wagons.

America's waterways were the most attractive measure in the early nineteenth century transportation. Their biggest drawback was that they flowed in one direction only. They were often too low in the autumn. They froze in the winter. They were remote from much desirable land. Consequently, overland road travel was important. No road was paved before 1790. Settlers had to fordwater courses, and ferries were both scarce and undependable. The western roads were worse than their eastern counterparts.

The Kentuckians were led by such men as William Henry Harrison into the Old Northwest, and the Tennesseans by Andrew Jackson and Sam Houston into the Gulf coastal plain. They were followed by New Englanders into the Mohawk and Hudson River valleys and Tidewater Virginians into the Ohio river valley.

Roads to the west were too far away and too expensive to construct. The federal government felt responsible for appropriating funds for military roads; otherwise, building roads was a task left to County and state governments.

There were four means of transport on America's waterway. The first was the canoe, a vessel hollowed out from the trunk of a tree about twenty feet long. Four men could build one in four days. Some were about thirty feet long. They were divided into four compartments. Paddlers sat in the front and back compartments. The cargo was in the two middle compartments. In order to improve speed, a square sail could be added.

A modified canoe was the pi-rogue. It was two canoes lashed together and floored over. It had a sail for motive power.

A flatboat had a flat bottom and was between twenty and a hundred feet long. Some had a small cabin and a barn for the passengers and their livestock. Oars were used for steering, and travel ended with nightfall because the crew could not see the water hazards. The flatboat was moored at river bank at night.

A keel boat was about fifty feet long and was seven to ten feet wide. It could carry twenty to forty tons of freight. Rowers and square sails propelled the keel boat. In turbulent waters, tow ropes were used. In shallow waters the vessel was propelled by poles. The keel boat could travel upstream.

The Louisiana Purchase in 1803 doubled the size of the country and opened the Mississippi River to the Gulf of Mexico without fees. Americans wanted internal improvements. The most notable advance in land travel in the United States in the nineteenth century was the turnpike. The roads were constructed by companies who financed the projects by selling shares to investors. Turnpikes were to connect population centers. They were all-weather roads and collected tolls from those who used them. They were a financial success.

The Capital Turnpike ran from Philadelphia to Lancaster, Pennsylvania. It was 24 feet wide, and arched to allow the water to drain off. The road bed was covered with a foot of rock and gravel. There were bridges on the Schuylkill, Great Brandywine, and Conestoga. The Rome-to-Geneva Turnpike opened in New York in 1800.

Zane's Trace connected Wheeling, West Virginia to Maysville, Kentucky, and then was extended to Nashville, Tennessee, in 1796. Trees were felled, but stumps were left in the roadway. Wagons were so very laden that they often became caught on the stumps. This situation gave rise to the expression, "I am stumped." It connected with a road to Lexington, Kentucky. The Natchez

Trace ran from Nashville, Tennessee to Natchez, Mississippi.

Americans' love with the turnpike was short lived. Two-way river traffic replaced overland travel with the invention of the steamboat. The first was the *New Orleans* of 371 tons built in Pittsburgh, Pennsylvania, in 1811. Steamboats required a minimum of only two feet of water to operate so vast stretches of the nation became accessible.

Besides advances in transportation and highway construction, another ingredient necessary for the western movement was the removal of the threat of Indian attack. At the battle of Tippecanoe in Indiana in 1811, William Henry Harrison led eight hundred American troops into battle against six thousand Shawnees led by the Prophet, the brother of Tecumseh. The pretext was the killing of an American sentinel. The two-hour battle ended with the Indians being driven from the field. The day afterwards Harrison destroyed their town. The battle of Tippecanoe dashed the hopes of an Indian confederacy. It destroyed the prestige of the Indian leadership. It hastened the outbreak of hostilities against Americans in the Old Northwest. It made Harrison's political reputation, and it secured Indiana Territory for settlement.

The War of 1812 demonstrated the necessity of road construction for national defense. Men and materiel had to be moved and moved quickly. Enlistments in the regular army were encouraged by the offer of bounty lands to veterans after the war. Congress selected reservations in the west where the veterans could locate their lands. The three reservations were in Illinois, Missouri, and Arkansas. Congress realized that locating veterans on the frontier would provide a defensive barrier to the east of which settlers would be willing to take the risk of purchasing public lands. The war led to the settlement of significant parts of Mississippi Territory, which included Alabama as well.

In 1815 the steamboat *Enterprise*, built at Brownsville, Pennsylvania, proved the feasibility of a return voyage from New Orleans. Steamboats came into their own and dominated river traffic for both passengers and freight. They revitalized traffic on the Great Lakes. The first steamers went only to Detroit. By 1835 there were regular schedules between Milwaukee and Chicago. Steamers carried passengers; sailing ships carried cargo.

With the best lands in valleys of eastern Tennessee, the Nashville Basin, the limestone area of Kentucky, and Ohio river lowlands already settled, Americans looked to go farther beyond. In New England, overcrowding and high prices combined to propel young families to move west. Land in New England was selling for $50 an acre, but in the West it sold for $2 or $3 per acre. Soil exhaustion in the Chesapeake caused Marylanders and Virginians to migrate. Thirteen counties in Maryland lost population between 1790 to 1800, as did twenty-six counties in Virginia. Improved transportation modes and routes also contributed to the migration.

Migrating was a late-winter event. Farmers sold their crops after the autumn harvest. The winter snowfall was melting, and the waterways had not become obstacles blocking access. Farmers needed to arrive in time to clear their land and plant their spring crops.

Kentucky, Tennessee, and Ohio were the destinations of choice of migrating Americans. They were among the ten most populous states in the nation in 1830. In 1840 Indiana joined them. In 1840 Buffalo, New York, had eight daily departures. Five years later, however, that number had dropped to three.

St. Louis became the focal point of river traffic. It was the gateway to the West at the confluence of the Ohio, Mississippi, and Missouri rivers.

Congress authorized funding of the National Road in 1809. It was originally called the

Cumberland Road because it began at Cumberland, Maryland. Construction began in 1811 on the 800-mile project. Construction was halted during the War of 1812. Thirteen miles had been built. Between 1815 and 1818 the most important section between Cumberland, Maryland, and Wheeling, West Virginia, opened. At Wheeling, traffic was diverted to the Ohio river. One could meet as many as a hundred teams a day headed toward Ohio. The Conestoga wagons had harnesses with bells on. Settlers moving west who experienced a break-down gave a bell to the one who repaired the damaged equipment which gave rise to the expression, "Arrived with bells on."

There were toll booths along the way for Americans moving west. Each booth had a pike, which it lowered across the roadway to prevent people from trying to drive around the booth without paying their toll. From that practice the term "turnpike" was coined.

In 1817 an estimated twenty-two thousand immigrants, the majority of whom came from Ireland where they could not find employment, arrived. The lure of cheap productive lands in the West caused immigrants to bypass the mills and factories in the East. Cities and towns in the East ceased to grow. A number of urban communities in the east actually lost population. In the southern states, where there was no interruption in annual cotton crops, the absence of crop rotations, and the failure to use fertilizers, the falling production prompted Americans to locate to Alabama, Mississippi, and Missouri.

Federal government funding of turnpikes and canals enhanced the settlement of transmontane America. Work on the National Road began at Zanesville, Ohio, in 1825. By 1833, it had reached Columbus, Ohio. Congress's last ante bellum appropriation was in 1838. In 1840 the states assumed control of constructing the road.

By 1850 the steamboat had put the National Road out of business. A steamboat could travel 15 to 25 miles an hour while a Conestoga wagon could make 3 to 5 miles in an hour. Travel by road did not revive itself until the 1870s, when the bicycle craze swept the nation.

The canal era dominated overland travel between 1820 and 1850. By 1840 the nation had 3,000 miles of canals. Canals led to the doubling of the population of New York City between 1820 and 1830 and allowed the Big Apple to surpass Philadelphia as the largest city in the nation. The Erie Canal bypassed Niagara Falls and followed the Mohawk Valley route, which was the natural egress through the Alleghenies. It opened in October 1825.

Between 1845 and 1848 improvements to the St. Lawrence allowed steamboat traffic. A hundred thousand people a year took passage on them. They averaged 50 miles a day. The trip from Albany to Buffalo, New York, took eight days. By land it took twenty days. By 1836 there were more than three thousand canal boats in operation.

In 1829 the Welland Canal connected Lake Erie and Lake Ontario, making passenger traffic available from Buffalo, New York; Cleveland, Ohio; Sandusky, Ohio; Toledo, Ohio; and Detroit, Michigan. It took fifteen days to go from Pittsburgh to the mouth of the Ohio.

Once the frontier crossed the Mississippi River, settlers were reluctant to go beyond the military posts, which sought to defend them against Indian incursions. The string of U.S. military posts built were Fort Howard, Wisconsin in 1816; Fort Winnebago in Wisconsin in 1828; Fort Snelling in Minnesota in 1820; Fort Atkinson, Kansas, in 1819; Fort Leavenworth, Kansas, in 1827, Fort Scott, Kansas, in 1842; Fort Gibson in Oklahoma in 1817; Fort Smith in Arkansas in 1827, and Fort Towson, Oklahoma, in 1824.

Florida

The first permanent European settlement in North America was St. Augustine, Florida established by the Spanish in 1565. Pensacola was established in 1698.

During the French and Indian War, the British captured Havana, Cuba, in 1762. At the Treaty of Paris in 1763, Spain agreed to trade Florida for Havana. The British created East Florida and West Florida. The Chattahoochee and Apalachicola rivers marked the boundary between them.

British rule ended in 1763 when Britain exchanged Florida for some islands in the Caribbean with Spain.

Bruno Rosselli, *The Italians in Colonial Florida: A Repertory of Italian Families Who Settled in Florida under the Spanish 1513-1762, 1784-1821, and British 1762-1784* (Jacksonville: Drew Press, 1948) covers the early Italians.

In 1767 Dr. Andrew Trumbull, who married a wealthy Greek wife, envisioned a utopian colony 60 miles south of St. Augustine on Mosquito Inlet. He called the settlement New Smyrna. He brought fifteen hundred colonists from Greece and Minorca. The colony was the largest single importation of foreigners into British North America. They were to produce silk and wine. The colony failed. The survivors revolted and moved to St. Augustine and to Georgia and South Carolina in 1773.

The Marquis de Lafayette visited the United States in 1824 and 1825. Congress recognized his contributions toward independence from Great Britain and awarded him a bounty land grant of more than 23,000 acres in Leon County, Florida. President John Quincy Adams issued the grant on 4 July 1825. Lafayette was also paid $200,000. Florida was admitted to the union in 1845. The Seminole Wars, 1835 to 1842, resulted in the tribe's removal from Florida to Oklahoma.

Kentucky

Kentucky was the fifteenth state to be admitted to the union in 1792 and was the first west of the Appalachian Mountains.

In 1750 Dr. Thomas Walker of Albemarle County, Virginia, explored the western part of the colony and discovered the gap in the mountains from Virginia into Kentucky. He named the gap after the younger son of King George, the Duke of Cumberland.

Daniel Boone explored the trans-Appalachian part of North America, after the French and Indian War between 1769 and 1772. Harrodsburg was the first permanent settlement in 1774. Boone returned to his home on the forks of the Yadkin River in upper North Carolina. He called his settlement Boonesborough, which was settled by North Carolinians in 1775. Harrodsburg, Kentucky, was settled by people from Virginia in 1775. James Harrod led the settlers 60 miles to the Ohio River and floated down the Ohio for 450 miles. Hancock Taylor from Orange County, Virginia, led others 750 miles down the Ohio to the falls of the Ohio and Elkhorn Creek. Capt. Thomas Bullitt in the spring of 1773 led the first expedition to make surveys awarded to veterans of the French and Indian War. With his company of forty men, he surveyed what would become the town of Louisville, named in honor of the King Louis of France for his support in the Revolutionary War. Bullitt returned to Fincastle County, Virginia, where the courthouse which had jurisdiction over Kentucky. Col. William Preston refused to record the surveys because no deputy surveyors had been involved; moreover, the lands had been reserved for the Indians rather than open to the colonists. Bullitt appealed to the royal governor and won. Many of the veteran settlers were aware that the Vandalia Land Company had claim to the lands on the east bank of the Kentucky River, so they split their claims by taking half on the east side of the river and half on the west.

The early settlers clung to the waterways. The early areas of settlement were along the Kentucky River, the Green River, the Blue Grass region, and Bear Grass. Those who came to Boonesborough, Harrodsburg, and St. Asaph came via the Cumberland Gap. Those at Boiling Spring and the Falls of the Ohio followed the Ohio River.

In 1774 the Indians under Chief Cornstalk were defeated at the battle of Point Pleasant in Lord Dunmore's War. With the Shawnee vanquished, the way was paved for the westward advance and settlement.

In 1775 Col. Richard Henderson of North Carolina purchased much of central Kentucky from the Cherokee in return for £2,000 pounds worth of trade goods. He commissioned Daniel Boone and others to blaze a trail into central Kentucky so that settlers could migrate to the area and purchase land from the Transylvania Company of Henderson. In 1776 Virginia abolished Fincastle County and organized Kentucky County to maintain the allegiance of the settlers in the west. Virginia gave every settler 400 acres. By 1780, migrations to Kentucky shifted from the Cumberland Gap in the southeastern corner to the Ohio river route, which caused northern Kentucky to grow rapidly. Between 1779 and 1780 twenty thousand people came to Kentucky.

Virginia offered bounty land to those Virginians who would clear the road over the Cumberland Mountains into Kentucky County in 1779. Kentucky bore the brunt of British inspired Indian attacks during the Revolutionary War. More people per capita died in Kentucky at the hands of the enemy than any other region of the young nation, and most of them did so after 1777.

During the Revolutionary War, from 1780 to 1782, fifty families from southern Pennsylvania and New Jersey made their way to Lincoln County, Kentucky, in the area that which became Henry, Shelby, and Mercer counties. They were Holland Dutch and French Huguenots. They included the Atens, Bantas, Bogarts, Bruners, Coverts, Van Arsdales, Vannuys, Demarest, Brewer, Bergen, Montford, Emots, Smock, Cassats, Cozines, Terhunes, Vories, and Bohons. Vincent Akers's *The Low Dutch Company* (Bargersville, N.Y.: Holland Society of New York, 1982) pertains to the settlement.

The early settlements in Kentucky were in the Bluegrass region along both sides of the Kentucky River. The settlers rejected eastern Kentucky on the Appalachian plateau. They remained south of the Ohio River because the Old Northwest was occupied by the Indians.

In the autumn of 1781 between five hundred and six hundred Virginia Baptists from Spotsylvania County headed toward their new Canaan in Kentucky. They traveled in a southwesterly direction to Lynchburg and Fort Chiswell, where they had to give up their wagons and load their goods on pack horses. They crossed the Holston, Clinch, and Powell rivers. They went through the Cumberland Gap. In the spring of 1782, they left Craig's fort and went to the Bluegrass plateau. The Rev. Lewis Craig was their leader. They formed the first Baptist congregation. It was located at South Elkhorn in Fayette County. George W. Ranck, "The Traveling Church: An Account of the Baptists from Virginia to Kentucky in 1781" (*The Register of the Kentucky Historical Society*, LXXIX (1981) 240-65).

In 1785 a large colony of Roman Catholics from Saint Mary's and Prince George's counties, Maryland migrated to Nelson County, Kentucky. They were also in Marion and

Washington counties and at Louisville. They traveled from Maryland to Pittsburgh in flatboats to Maysville, Kentucky. Among the families were Abell, Boone, Bowles, Cissell, Dant, Edelin, Hayden, Howard, Luckett, Lancaster, Mattingly, Miles, Mudd, Nally, Rapier, Smith, Spalding, Thompson, and Wathen. More families followed them in 1786, 1787, 1788, 1790, and 1791. The first priest arrived in 1787.

About ninety percent of the inhabitants of Kentucky in 1790 had migrated there via the Wilderness Road. Robert Lee Kincaid's *The Wilderness Road* (New York: The Dobbs Merill Company, 1967) gives a history of it.

When Kentucky became a state in 1792, there were five hundred stills in operation. The cash crop was corn, but it was too bulky to be transported back across the mountains to markets in the East. In order to repay the Revolutionary War debt, eastern politicians enacted legislation for a tax on the commodity of whiskey. The burden was disproportionally borne by people in the west. The law led to the Whiskey Rebellion in western Pennsylvania and a mass exodus of farmers to Kentucky in 1794. The treaty of Greenville in 1795 effectively ended the Indian raids into Kentucky. By the time of the 1800 federal census the population had increased to 179,873. By the time of the War of 1812, Kentucky had two thousand stills. They were concentrated in the counties of Fayette, Scott, Franklin, Jessamine, Anderson, Mercer, Marion, and Daviess.

By 1808 the Pope created four new sees. They were: Boston, New York City, Philadelphia, and Bardstown, Kentucky, where the first cathedral west of the Alleghenies in English-speaking America was erected.

Tennessee
Like Gaul, Tennessee is divided into three parts: East, Middle, and West. These divisions are natural geographic ones. East Tennessee is an upland, often mountainous area. Middle Tennessee consists of gentle foothills, limestone basins, and fertile grasslands. West Tennessee is a low loess soil plain. Tennessee is adjacent to eight other states, viz. Virginia, Kentucky, Arkansas, Missouri, North Carolina, Mississippi, Alabama, and Georgia, so it plays a major role in the westward migration. No other state has such a geographical asset.

After the French and Indian and Revolutionary wars, Tennessee and Kentucky were the two states which were the destinations for the westward movement of the population. The first settlers entered the area in 1769; they were from North Carolina and Virginia. William Bean and his Scots-Irish neighbors came from Pittsylvania County, Virginia. Their settlement was in East Tennessee in the Watauga River valley, and they banded together to form the Watauga Association in 1771. There were four settlements. One was north of the Holston River near Bristol. The river took its name from Stephen Holston of Virginia who came there in 1758. The next was along the Watauga river near Elizabethton. The third was west of the Holsteinriver near Rogersville in Carter's valley, and the fourth along the Nolichucky River near Erwin.

Some of the settlers located there because they had participated in the Regulator War in a rebellion against the last royal governor.

In 1776 North Carolina organized the aforementioned settlements as part of her western territory as Washington County, North Carolina. Colonists uneasy about declaring themselves independent from England also sought refuge in Tennessee and as far away from the fighting as possible. The Washington County, North Carolina, court minutes reveal that the court spent much of its time on cases of persons charged with being Loyalists or of harboring Loyalists. Loyalists were imprisoned, and Tories had their property confiscated and were exiled. Still others were glad to be free from the Royal Proclamation of 1763, which prohibited settlement beyond the mountains. Central Tennessee was settled in 1779 with the founding of Nashville. Three hundred settlers made their way to French Lick on the Cumberland river. James Robertson led a group along the Wilderness Road to the Cumberland Gap. They traveled across Kentucky and then descended into the Sumner and Davidson County area. Others floated down the Tennessee river to Muscle Shoals and up the Ohio and Cumberland to the Red River where Fort Nashborough was. The battle of Kings Mountain in 1780, the turning point of the war in the South, had a number of volunteers from Tennessee. In fact, all the American troops at King's Mountain were militia. There were no Continental Army personnel present. There were 78 Americans killed and 62 wounded. The British lost 157, and another 153 were wounded. The Americans took 706 prisoners. Many patriots sought refuge in Tennessee following the taking of Charleston and the invasion of North Carolina by the British.

The settlers in East Tennessee kept the road open to Kentucky and assured that the settlements there would continue. George Rogers Clark's conquest of the Illinois country made it possible.

The Nashville Road opened in 1788. The Old Walton Road opened in 1795. Both gave access to the Cumberland settlements in the most fertile part of the state. In two months in 1796, twenty-six thousand settlers crossed to Nashville.

In 1784 North Carolina ceded the area to the United States in order to secure federal protection for the area. The United States refused the offer, and the settlers organized the state of Franklin, named in honor of Benjamin Franklin whose support they hoped to enlist. It lasted but four years until North Carolina regained control in 1789. The Tar Heel State ceded the area again to the federal government, and it was organized as the Territory South of the River Ohio. Kentucky was on its northern border. In 1790 Tennessee had a population of 35,691. Tennessee grew more slowly than Kentucky and achieved statehood four years after Kentucky, in 1796, as the sixteenth state in the union. The capital was Knoxville.

North Carolina had introduced a bounty land system to encourage enlistments during the Revolutionary War and established a military reservation in the upper half of Middle Tennessee.

In 1798 the Cherokee Indians ceded land along the Clinch and Tennessee rivers. Other cessions followed. With the defeat of the Creek Indians at the battle of Horseshoe Bend in 1814, Andrew Jackson negotiated with the Chickasaw to extend the boundary of the state from the west fork of the Tennessee river to the Mississippi river. In 1820 the rich, western third of the state between the west bank of the west fork of the Tennessee and the east bank of the Mississippi was opened for settlement. Memphis became the most important city between St. Louis and New Orleans.

During the Creek War of 1813 to 1814, Gov. William Blount called for three thousand five hundred volunteers. John Cocke led one of the two armies, and Andrew Jackson recruited another thousand men from West Tennessee. John Coffee had a cavalry force of thirteen hundred. The outcome of the war was that there would not be any Indian confederation.

After the Civil War, a hundred and four Welsh families from Pennsylvania migrated to Knoxville to work in the mining industry.

Chapter Eight: The Old Northwest

The Old Northwest encompassed the present day states of Ohio, Indiana, Illinois, Michigan, Wisconsin and part of Minnesota.

The French were the first Europeans to settle there. Berthold Fernow's *The Ohio Valley in Colonial Days* (New Orleans: Polyanthos, 1978) relates the settlement of the early pioneers. They had settlements at Vincennes, Indiana; Cahokia, Kaskaskia, and Peoria, Illinois; Prairie du Chien and Green Bay, Wisconsin; and Detroit and Michilimackinac, Michigan. The United States acquired the area at the Treaty of Paris that concluded the Revolutionary War. It became necessary to validate the private claims to lands under the previous French and British governments before the United States opened the area to settlement. The machinery of government came with legislation in 1784 and 1785, culminating in the Northwest Ordinance in 1787. The ordinance outlined the territorial form of government, created a new land system, and provided a pathway for new states to enter the Union.

No more than five and no fewer than three states were to be carved out of the Northwest Territory. An area had to have a population of sixty thousand before applying for statehood. It imposed a rectangular survey system of the land and eliminated indiscriminate surveys in lieu of the metes and bounds of realty. It also cancelled the lottery system. Settlers could purchase land directly from the federal government. The first sales were to land companies, which in turn resold the land on more favorable terms to individuals. The minimum purchase was a section of 640 acres.

Access to the Old Northwest came in 1806 with the National Road, the first federally-supported road in the nation. Baltimore, Maryland, was its eastern terminus, but construction actually began at Cumberland. Although building contracts were let in 1811, construction did not began until later. The cost was $13,000 a mile. The road was 30 feet wide in the mountains and sixty-six feet elsewhere. Bridges were to be constructed out of solid masonry. The center was to be raised with a ditch on both sides to drain off the water. The roadbed consisted of crushed stone.

By 1818 the road was completed to Wheeling, West Virginia. The second phase was funded in 1825. The road was 591 miles long and ultimately stretched from Cumberland, Maryland, to Vandalia, Illinois, in 1840 at a cost of $6,824,919.33. The National Road suffered from melting snow and heavy rains. The eastern portion wore out before the western portion was completed. President James Monroe vetoed legislation which would have authorized the federal government to collect tolls for improvements and repairs. In the early 1830s, Congress turned over the road to the states through which it ran.

The National Road was the nation's busiest land artery to the west. It slipped into a long decline with the coming of the railroads near the middle of the nineteenth century.

Freighting and coaching companies arose to handle the transportation business. Stage coaches were pulled by four horses. They were changed about every twelve miles. By 1837 the journey from Washington to St. Louis took ninety-four hours.

Ohio

The first settlement in Ohio in the southeastern quadrant above the Ohio River was at Marietta, Ohio, which was named for Marie Antoinette, Queen of France. The founders of the

Ohio Company were officers and men who served in Continental Line units from Massachusetts, Rhode Island, and Connecticut. These New Englanders met at the Bunch of Grapes Tavern in Boston in 1786 at the invitation of Gen. Rufus Putnam and Gen. Benjamin Tupper. Their agents were the Rev. Manasseh Cutler of Salem, Massachusetts, and Winthrop Sargent. The town of Marietta was laid out in 1786, and the settlers began arriving two years later. Fourteen of them were from Boston, Middletown, Brookfield, Chester, Conway, Rutland, Westborough, and Chesterfield in Massachusetts. Sixteen were from Colchester, Canaan, Lyme, Lebanon, North Lyme, Saybrook, and Middletown, Connecticut. The Marietta Land Office opened in 1800.

The Ohio Enabling Act of 1802, which was modified the following year, provided that five percent of the proceeds of Ohio Land sales be dedicated to roads. Three percent of that amount was for inside Ohio and two percent for those coming to Ohio's borders. Ohio used the funds to connect Lake Erie and the Ohio river.

The United States followed their colonial example and established the Military District in the Northwest Territory to encourage seasoned veterans to locate on the vulnerable frontier. The bounty land program of the Continental Congress used the land in trans-Appalachia as a means of remuneration to those who enlisted and remained in the service. Between 1783 and 1855, some 60 million acres were allocated to some five hundred fifty thousand veterans, their widows, and minor heirs.

Ohio encompassed the corn belt north of the Ohio river. It was accessible via the Scioto, Miami, and Wabash River Valleys. By the 1850s, better plows had been invented. The Corn Belt extended from Ohio to Iowa.

Another New England enclave in northeastern Ohio was the Western Reserve. Under the grant made by King Charles II in 1662, Connecticut received all land between its northern and southern borders extending as far westward as possible. Connecticut sought to assert her claim in the middle of the seventeenth century. She selected the Wyoming valley in northeastern Pennsylvania. The Susquehannah Company purchased the land from the Indians in 1754. Pennsylvania insisted that the land claimed by Connecticut was hers. A national court ruled in Pennsylvania's favor in 1792. Connecticut simply laid claim to land west of Pennsylvania. Eventually Connecticut ceded this land to the federal government except for a 120 twenty mile strip. In 1786 the Ohio Land Company led many Massachusetts residents to migrate to the Buckeye State.

In 1794 Gen. Anthony Wayne defeated the Indians and the British at the Battle of Fallen Timbers. By the Treaty of Greenville, the Indians relinquished approximately half of this land. In 1795 Connecticut quit-claimed over two-thirds of the tract, which was east of the Cuyahoga River, to the Connecticut Land Company. The company sent out Moses Cleveland to survey the tract. While migration to the tract was slow, there were thirty-five settlements in a hundred and three townships. There were one thousand three hundred and two people in the area. Plymouth was named for those from Plymouth, Connecticut, Norwalk for those from Norwalk, Connecticut, and Greenwich for those from Greenwich, Long Island, New York.

Congress in 1796 set aside a tract known as the United States Military District in the central part of the Ohio east of the Scioto river. It encompassed the counties of Coshocton, Delaware, Franklin, Guernsey, Holmes, Knox, Licking, Morrow, Muskingum, Noble, and Tuscarawas.

In 1800 Connecticut surrendered its sovereignty to the Western Reserve in return for federal recognition of its land grants. The area became Trumbull County, Northwest Territory.

During the Revolutionary War, the British, assisted by Benedict Arnold, had ravaged the coast of Connecticut. The British Navy wrought destruction on the towns of New Haven, Greenwich, Fairfield, Norwalk, and New London. Connecticut set aside about a half million acres at the western end of the Western Reserve as compensation to people and institutions in 1792. The tract became known as the Firelands and embraced the counties of Erie and Huron. Deeds for the land these sufferers received were to be recorded in the town where their properties were burned in the bombardment.

The Seven Ranges were the most accessible federal lands in Ohio and were the first the federal government offered for sale at the cost of $2 per acre. In contrast, Connecticut offered land in the Western Reserve for $.50 an acre. Steubenville, Ohio, was the first settlement in the Seven Ranges. Most of the settlers were Germans from Centre County and earlier from Lancaster County, Pennsylvania. The Steubenville Land Office opened in 1800.

To protect the approaches to Marietta, Ohio, the Ohio Land Company gave a hundred acres to males aged 18 and above who promised to carry a gun in exchange. This Donation Tract was in Washington and Morgan Counties.

In southwestern Ohio was the Symmes Purchase. In 1795 John Cleves Symmes, a justice of the Supreme Court of New Jersey, purchased 311,682 acres for $.67 per acre. His employees kept poor record of sales and prompted a Congressional investigation during which Symmes's cabin containing the records burned. Most of the early settlers were from Salem, Gloucester, and Burlington counties, New Jersey. The Symmes Purchase covered Preble, Butler, Hamilton, Warren, and Greene Counties.

Virginia promised bounty land in Ohio to its veterans in the event that its land south of the Green River in Kentucky proved insufficient. It was opened to veterans of the Continental Line but not Virginia State Line or militia veterans. It embraced the counties of Adams, Brown, Clermont, Clinton, Fayette, Highland, Madison, Union, and portions of Champaign, Clark, Delaware, Franklin, Greene, Hardin, Logan, Marion, Pickaway, Pike, Ross, Scioto, and Warren Counties. The Virginia lands were measured by metes and bounds and not the rectangular survey scheme for federal lands.

Refugees from the French Revolution fled to the United States. Many were swindled out of their money by a land company that had no land. Congress compensated them with 24,000 acres in Scioto County in 1795 and 1798, known as the French Grants.

Besides Connecticut, Virginia claimed all of the Old Northwest and had instituted a plan of rewarding her Continental forces with bounty land north of the Ohio. Virginia kept the area between the Little Miami and Scioto rivers. The military bounty land warrants could take any shape the grantee desired so long as the boundaries did not overlap with a prior claimant. The bounty land tract included Scioto, Adams, Clermont, Warren, Ross, Fairfield, and Franklin Counties. By 1852 Virginia had satisfied all of the claims for about four million acres due the veterans and their heirs and ceded the unclaimed lands to the federal government. Most veterans sold their warrants to speculators rather than move out to Ohio to settle on the land.

Three separate tracts of one mile square were issued to Ebenezer Zane in 1796 on the condition that he open a road from Wheeling, West Virginia, to the Ohio River at Maysville, Kentucky. Zanesville on the Muskingum River, Lancaster on the Hocking River, and Chillicothe on the east bank of the Scioto linked together a route for Kentuckians to reach Pickaway and Fairfield counties, Ohio. Virginians and Pennsylvanians followed on their heels.

In recognition of aid given by Canadians during the Revolutionary War, Congress set aside 50,086 acres of land known as the Refugee Tract in 1798. The land was in Franklin, Licking, Fairfield, and Perry counties. Claimants had to have lived in Canada before 4 July 1776, and had been forced to flee their homes because of aid given to Americans, and had not returned to Canada prior to 25 November 1783. There were sixty-seven claimants.

General Anthony Wayne drove the Indians out of Ohio. By the treaty of Greenville in 1795, more than half of Ohio was opened to settlement. The eleventh category of settlers to locate in Ohio was the United States Military District established in 1796. Revolutionary War military veterans in Continental service took their bounty land within the district so that Ohio has more Revolutionary War veterans buried in its soil than any other state.

The increase in population in Ohio was impressive. Between 1820 and 1840 her population tripled. They were largely farmers. One acre of corn yielded three to six times as much grain as one of wheat. One kernel of corn produced 150 to 300 kernels. Corn and wheat were too difficult to transport, so the settlers opted for pigs and whiskey instead.

Cincinnati, the Queen of the West, replaced Charleston, South Carolina, as the sixth largest city in the nation about 1810. Its principal industry was pork packing. Its first packing house opened in 1818. In 1838 some 182,000 swine were packed.

Settlers from Bath County, Virginia, migrated to Gallia, Muskingham, and Hocking counties. Delaware and Fairfield counties were the choices of Virginians from Hardy and Pendleton counties. The Finns in Ohio are treated in John Imari Kolehmainen's *"Founding of Finnish Settlements in Ohio"* (in *Ohio State Archaeology and Historical Quarterly* XLIX (1938),150-159).

Indiana

The earliest settlement in Indiana was about 1731 when the French built a fort at Vincennes. The British ousted the French in the French and Indian War in 1763. The Americans seized Vincennes in 1778, lost it in 1779, and retook it in 1779. George Rogers Clark took the Old Northwest on behalf of Virginia. Illinois County was set up. After the war, a permanent settlement was made at Clarksville in 1784. The gore in Dearborn County was the third settlement in the state.

Anthony Wayne was victorious over the Indians in 1794 and built Fort Wayne to protect the northern exposure. In 1800 Indiana Territory was created. Prior to that date, the only land in private hands were the French grantees at Vincennes. From 1779 to 1783 the Vincennes Court granted land in 400-acre tracts to Americans who wanted land. By the end of Revolutionary War 26,000 acres had been granted. Virginians who served under George Rogers Clark received bounty land. The Illinois or Clark's Grants were in Clark, Floyd, and Scott counties. In 1800 the population of Indiana was 2,500. In 1803 wine-growing families from France settled on 2,500 acres. They increased their holdings by buying another 1,200 acres. The United States opened the Vincennes Land Office in 1804.

George Rapp from Iptingen, Germany, acquired 5,000 acres west of Pittsburgh. The first three hundred arrived in 1804. His settlement was called Harmony. It was in Butler County. In 1814 they sold out and settled in New Harmony, Posey County.

70

William Henry Harrison led eight hundred soldiers against six thousand Shawnee who were led by the Prophet, the brother of Tecumseh, at the battle of Tippecanoe 7 November 1811. The strike was made because an American sentinel had been killed. In the two-hour battle, Harrison drove the Indians from the field and secured Indiana for settlement. The battle dashed the hopes of an Indian confederation. It also destroyed the prestige of the Indian leadership. It made Harrison's reputation and secured Indiana Territory for white settlers.

In 1815 there were 64,000 people in Indiana. Indiana's tremendous growth in population occurred between 1820 and 1840 when her population quadrupled. The state became known as the Crossroads of America. The National Road linked Indianapolis and Vandalia, Illinois.

In 1816 warrants were issued to Canadian volunteers who were citizens of the United States before the War of 1812 and had joined the forces of the United States as volunteers.

In the 1830s the northern part of Indiana was settled because it was accessible via the Wabash and Erie canals.

New Englanders began arriving in the mid-nineteenth century and settled in the northern part of the state.

German settlers appear in William A. Fritsch's *German Settlers and Settlement in Indiana*. (Evansville, Ind. 1915).

Quakers opposed to slavery migrated from Tennessee and the Carolinas to Randolph and Wayne Counties. Their records are in Willard C. Heiss's *Encyclopedia of American Quaker Genealogy* (Indianapolis, Indiana: Indiana Historical Society, in seven parts of vol. VII),

Switzerland County was named for its early Swiss settlers as related in Perret Dufour's *The Swiss Settlement of Switzerland County, Indiana* (Indianapolis: Indiana Historical Commission, 1925).

Illinois

The French established their first permanent settlement at Cahokia in 1699 followed by Kaskaskia in 1703. The British gained control after the French and Indian War in 1763. Many of the French settlers withdrew to St. Louis, Missouri; Natchez, Mississippi; and other towns not under British control. George Rogers Clark captured the area during the Revolutionary War. Some of his men and their families settled at Bellefontaine in 1779. Virginia ceded Illinois to the United States in 1784. The Ohio River Valley brought settlers from North Carolina, Virginia, Maryland, Kentucky, and Tennessee.

More Virginians settled at New Design in 1786 and 1793. In 1797 Rev. Daniel Badgley organized a Baptist church at New Design, Illinois. The settlers in the town were Virginians.

Illinois Territory was created in 1809. Its first land office was at the capital, Kaskaskia. Most of the settlers prior to the War of 1812 were Southerners. The Missouri Compromise of 1820-1821 diverted potential settlers with slaves. People from New York and New England did not arrive in any significant numbers until the opening of the Erie Canal about 1825.

In 1817 and 1818, Morris Birkbeck and George Flower established an English settlement in Edwards County. Flower called his community Albion. Birkbeck died in 1825 when he was trying to swim across a flooded river. When his body was found, he still had his umbrella in his hand like a proper Englishman.

Ferdinand Ernst established a group of Europeans in Vandalia, Fayette County. There were about a hundred Germans. They had landed at the port of Baltimore and arrived in Vandalia in December 1819. Paul E. Stroble, Jr.'s *High on the Okaw's Western Bank, Vandalia, Illinois, 1819-1839* (University of Illinois, 1992) chronicles the early history.

In 1817, the War of 1812 bounty-land tract between the Mississippi and Illinois rivers opened. It contained 3,500,000 acres and encompassed fourteen counties and parts of four others. They were Adams, Brown, Calhoun, Fulton, Hancock, Henderson, Knox, McDonough, Mercer, Peoria, Pike, Schuyler, Stark, and Warren. It also included parts of Bureau, Henry, Marshall, and Putnam Counties. Of the three military tracts opened to veterans, the Illinois tract attracted the most interest. When Illinois attained statehood in 1818, it agreed not to tax the military bounty lands for five years. The distribution of lots was by means of a lottery, which kept veterans from knowing what the lands they were to receive looked like.

Construction began on the Erie Canal in 1818. Steamship traffic began on the Great Lakes and offered service from Buffalo to Detroit. Indian cessions in 1819 and 1821 opened Michigan for settlement by Americans. The canal opened in 1825. The road through the Kalamazoo Valley opened in 1829.

In the early 1800s, the military recognized that the Great Sauk Trail might be the best route between Detroit and Chicago. Pioneers in the thousands followed it to the West. The discovery of lead at Galena, along with agriculture, drew settlers to Illinois. The first mining lease was granted in 1822. Col. James Johnson brought twenty miners and four dozen slaves from Kentucky to work his claim. The town of Galena was laid out in 1826. By 1845 Galena shipped 54,494,850 pounds of lead. It was the busiest port between St. Paul and St. Louis. Halfway between Chicago and Galena was Rockford, founded in 1834.The Chicago Road was an important route served by two stage departures from Detroit and Chicago.

In 1827 more than four hundred men from Sangamon and Morgan counties enrolled to serve in the Winnebago War. The Black Hawk War had ten thousand eight hundred Illinois veterans. The Americans defeated the Sac and Fox Indians. Veterans who served in the northern part of the state saw how rich the soil was and began to relocate there after the Indians had been removed.

The Black Hawk War of 1832 resulted in the cession of the Sac and Fox Indians. Not only Illinois but also Iowa had thousands of acres opened for settlement. In 1833 a strip of 9,000 square miles was opened along the west bank of the Mississippi River. Pioneers poured into the area and founded Dubuque, Davenport, and Burlington, Iowa.

In 1834 Cleng Peerson founded the first Norwegian settlement in the Midwest 12 miles northeast of Ottawa, Illinois. There were six families in the initial group. More joined them in 1834 and 1842. A. E. Strand's *A History of the Norwegians of Illinois, A Concise Record of the Struggles and Achievements of the Early Settlers Together with a Narrative of What is now Being Done by Norwegian-Americans in the Development of Their Adopted Country with the Valuable Collaboration of Numerous Authors and Contributors* (1905) discusses this Scandinavian group. In 1834 there were two hundred thirty-five exiles. Twenty-six others joined them later. *Vide* Ernst W. Olson, *Swedish Element in Illinois* (Chicago: Swedish American Biographical Association, 1917) and *History of the Swedes in Illinois* (Chicago: Egeberg-Holmberg, 1908). In 1838 the National Road reached Vandalia, Illinois, which was the second state capital.The Mormons came to the state in 1839 and founded Nauvoo.

Settlement in the northern half of Illinois was much later than in the southern half of the state and along the Mississippi River. While the absence of trees eliminated the need for labor for girdling and felling trees, it was necessary to have a four oxen team to pull a plow through the prairie soil. In addition the lack of lumber made it difficult to build homes and barns or to find fuel.

By the 1840 federal census the transportation routes accounted for half of the Illinois' inhabitants being from New York, New England, and Germany. Between the 1820 and 1840 federal censuses, the population of Illinois grew more than eightfold.

John Deere, a native of Vermont, began studying the trade of a blacksmith in 1825 and came to Illinois 1836. The soil turned by a New England plow would not perform adequately in the rich soil of the northwest. Deere discovered that plows made of steel were not affected and were safe. Within a decade he had made 1,000 steel plows.

In 1846 Eric Janson, a Swede who insisted that the Bible alone be used exclusively in matters of faith, abandoned the Lutheran Church. He brought one thousand five hundred adherents to Bishop Hill in Henry County, Illinois. He was murdered when he attempted to stop a woman follower with her husband from leaving the colony. In time the Jansonists became Methodists and spread into Knox County.

In 1848 the Illinois-Michigan Canal opened.

In 1849 Protestant exiles from Madeira immigrated from Portugal to Springfield and Jacksonville, Illinois.

In 1851 a Roman Catholic priest, Father Charles Chiniquy, quarreled with his superiors. He led a thousand of his communicants to set up a Presbyterian Church at Ste. Anne, Illinois.

Southern Illinois reflected that half of the state was an extension of southern culture, religion, and agriculture. Accordingly, there were two hundred fifty-five thousand men from Illinois who served in the Confederacy.

Michigan

Michigan was originally part of New France. The French used it as a base for the fur trade. Its first permanent settlement was Sault Ste. Marie in 1668 made by Jacques Marquette. The second settlement was at Fort Pontchartrain in 1701. It was later renamed Detroit. Christian Denissen's *Genealogy of the French Families of the Detroit River Region 1701-1936* (Detroit Society for Genealogical Research, 1976) covers two centuries of French settlers.

The French lost Michigan to the British in the French and Indian War in 1763. It was incorporated into Quebec in 1774. During the Revolutionary War, the English from Michigan raided the settlements in Kentucky. The United States gained control of the area in 1783 at the end of the Revolutionary War. The British, however, continued to occupy their forts in Detroit and Michilmackinaw until Gen. Anthony Wayne drove them out in 1796. Mary Napolka's *The Polish Immigrants* in *Detroit* to *1914* (Chicago, 1946) and James J. Tye's *The Detroit Poles, Comprehensive Bibliography and Compendium* (author, 1975) cover this Slavic element.

During the War of 1812, the British captured Detroit, but the Americans retook the city and fort in 1813.

Indian cessions followed in 1819 and 1821. Steamship travel between Buffalo and Detroit on Lake Erie greatly increased settlement in Michigan. In 1829 a road through Kalamazoo Valley in 1829 and the completion of the Chicago Road in 1835 also enabled New Englanders, New

Yorkers, and Europeans to reach the state. Charles A. Flagg's *An Index of Pioneers from Massachusetts to the West, Especially the State of Michigan* (Baltimore: Genealogical Publishing Co., 1975) is noteworthy. Immigrants, attracted by the lumber and mining industries, made their way to Michigan.

The Dutch are treated in Adrian Van Koevering's *Legends of the Dutch; the Story of a Mass Movement of 19ᵗʰ Century Pilgrims* (Grand Rapids: Reformed Press, 1923.) and Aleida J. Pieters's *A Dutch Settlement in Michigan.* (Columbia University Ph.D. dissertation, 1923). Mika Roinila's *Finland Swedes in Michigan* (Michigan State University Press, 2012) and S. Ilmonen's *The History of Finnish Americans: Finnish Settlements in the United States and Canada*, (Salt Lake City: Finnish Publications Family Sleuths, 1998.) cover Michigan's Finns.

Wisconsin

Like Michigan, Wisconsin was part of New France. The French had a trading post there as early as 1648 but lost the area at the end of the French and Indian War in 1763 to the British. Wisconsin became part of the U.S. in 1783, and part of the Northwest Territory in 1787; however, military control over the territory remained in British hands until the end of the War of 1812. It became part of the Northwest Territory in 1787. New Englanders and New Yorkers, along with immigrants from northern Europe, contributed most of the settlers.

The discovery of the lead district, which stretched form Galena, Illinois, to Mineral Point, Wisconsin in the southern part of the state attracted 1,600 miners by 1826. In the 1830s, the towns of Milwaukee, Racine, and Kenosha were settled.

Between 1839 and 1843, Lutherans from Pomerania, Brandenburg, and Saxony came to Wisconsin as explained in Lieslotte Clemens' *Old Lutheran Emigration from Pomerania to the U.S.A.* (Kiel, Germany: Pomerania Foundation, 1976). Richard H. Zeitlin's *Germans in Wisconsin* (Madison: State Historical Society, 2000) covers the state. Poles came to Wisconsin as treated in Frank H. Miller's *The Polanders in Wisconsin* (Milwaukee, 1896).

Minnesota

In 1848 the last of the Indian lands in Minnesota were relinquished, resulting in the biggest influx of settlers. Fort Snelling near St. Paul was the first permanent settlement with steamboat service on the Mississippi River. The Chippewa and Sioux ceded their lands in 1837, opening the St. Croix valley for the lumber industry.

The rush to Minnesota was spectacular in the 1850s. Land was occupied much faster than it could be surveyed. Between 1850 and 1857, the population increased by 2,400 percent or an increase of 144,000 persons.

Algot E. Strand's *A History of the Swedish Americans of Minnesota* (Chicago: Lewis Publishing Company, 1910) treats one of the many Scandinavian ancestors.

Chapter Nine: The Old Southwest

As Dorothy Potter has written, "The 'Old Southwest' is loosely defined as part of the early American southern territory ruled at different times by Spanish, French, and British colonial governments." Prior to European settlement, the "Old Southwest" had been home to the Creek, Cherokee, Choctaw, and Chickasaw Nations. For Spanish occupiers in particular, these tribes formed an important barrier to British colonial advance. The "Old Southwest" in its entirety lay east of the Mississippi River, so once it became American territory, following the Revolutionary War, it would encompass the future states of Alabama, Mississippi, and portions of Louisiana and Florida.

Genealogists searching for ancestors in the "Old Southwest" prior to statehood can avail themselves of two important source record collections. Once the territory came under American control, landholders were required to file proof of ownership with their new government. These proofs are found in Series VIII and IX of the 38-volume collection, the American State Papers, which can be found online. The majority of settlers in the "Old Southwest" prior to statehood came from the British colonies–even when the area was under foreign domination. As Mrs. Potter has written, these individuals "were required to obtain passports for passage through Indian or foreign-held territory from roughly 1770 to 1820." Mrs. Potter has assembled these records in her fully-indexed book, *Passports of Southeastern Pioneers, 1770-1823, Indian, Spanish and other Land Passports for Tennessee, Kentucky, Georgia, Mississippi, Virginia, North, and South Carolina.*

Alabama

Mobile was the first permanent European settlement established by the French in 1702. France lost its colony to the British following the French and Indian War. During the French regime, colonists from South Carolina and Georgia arrived. English as well as French and Spanish colonists came from Europe.

British colonists with strong British sympathies left Georgia for Alabama in 1775. More planters from North Carolina, South Carolina, and Georgia followed in 1783. The British lost Mobile to the Spanish at the Peace of Paris in 1783.

Alabama, above the 31st parallel, became part of Mississippi in 1795. The Tennessee Valley in the northern part of the state was settled in 1809. There were 16,000 whites and 22,624 blacks in Alabama. A decade later in 1819 there were 99,198 whites and 47,665 blacks.

The Louisiana Purchase necessitated an overland route to the Southwest to link Washington, D.C., to New Orleans, Louisiana. The horse path would facilitate the mail, and service began in 1806. Travelers along the route had to have passports to cross the Creek Nation. The Creeks had the sole right to operate the inns and way stations on the path. The path meant that Georgians were the most numerous settlers in southern Alabama. In 1810 the Federal Road was widened to move troops and wagons in the event of a war. The numbers of pioneers led to the clash of cultures in the Creek War of 1813 to 1814. Henry deLeon Southerland's, *The Federal*

Road through Georgia, the Creek Nations, and Alabama, 1806-1836 (Tuscaloosa: University of Alabama, 1989) describes the thoroughfare between 1806 and 1836.

The purchase of lands in northern Alabama became possible when the land office in Nashville, Tennessee opened in 1811. It moved to Huntsville, Alabama, in 1812. Between October 1811 and March 1812 there were 233 vehicles and 3,726 people who crossed the Flynt River in Georgia headed westward.

The Muskogee Nation occupied much of Georgia and southern Alabama. Americans referred to them as the "Creek" because of their skill in traversing the creeks and settling along the creeks. Chief Red Eagle led about four thousand Creeks, who were known as the Red Sticks because they painted their bodies and war clubs red. He sought to prevent further encroachment on the Creek lands. The northern Shawnee chief, Tecumseh, visited the area and made an alliance with the Red Sticks.

Late in 1812, the Red Sticks slaughtered two white families. The Red Creek faction attacked Fort Mims along the Alabama River and slew between two hundred forty-five and two hundred sixty persons. They took more than a hundred women, children, and slaves as prisoners. The atrocities were avenged by Andrew Jackson, who led a force of five thousand militia men who had assembled at Fayetteville, Tennessee to save Huntsville, Alabama. His forces captured the Creek villages of Tallushatchee south of Huntsville and Talladega. At the battle of Horseshoe Bend, eight hundred warriors died. Jackson forced the Indians to surrender sites for military roads and posts and to cede much of their lands. Jackson forced the Indians to cede 23 million acres. For his victory, Jackson became a major general in the regular army. Andrew Jackson led his men in the capture of Pensacola and Mobile in November 1814, before advancing on New Orleans. Jackson looked like a military genius.

Bonapartists were the subject of persecution following the restoration of the monarchy in France. About one thousand five hundred exiles sought refuge in the United States in 1816. They arrived in Philadelphia in the winter. Refugees from the slave insurrection in San Domingo arrived at the same time. They selected a new home in Marengo County, Alabama. They traveled by sea from Philadelphia to Mobile in 1817. Congress gave them four townships in the Creek Cession. They called their settlement Demopolis. It was at the confluence of the Tombigbee and Black Warrior rivers. The new immigrants believed that Alabama had a climate similar to France. The Vine and Olive Company colony was not a success. They were required to make a settlement within three years, plant one acre in each quarter in vines within seven years, and plant five hundred olive trees within seven years. When they had their lands surveyed, they learned that the lands where they were living were not theirs. Many moved away and founded Arcola. They brought in German redemptioners, who proved to be successful farmers, after completing the terms of their contracts. Some of the French left to colonize Galveston, Texas. A storm destroyed their settlement and scattered them along the Gulf coast. Some returned to Philadelphia. Others drifted to Mobile. Rafe Blaufarb's *Bonapartists in the Border Lands: French Exiles and Refugees on the Golf Coasts, 1815-1735* (Tuscaloosa: University of Alabama, 2005) treats them.

Alabama's population increased by 1,000 percent between 1810 and 1820. In 1816, one traveler counted four thousand immigrants on his nine-day journey across Alabama. Several factors accounted for this phenomenon. The Americans had been pushed out of the Piedmont due to poor economic conditions and exhausted soil. Federal lands sold for $2 an acre with a minimum purchase of 640 acres. The price of cotton paid by the milling English was favored by the rich soil and the navigable rivers.

The routes to the Old Southwest included the Natchez Trace, which ran from Nashville, Tennessee, to Natchez, Mississippi. Farmers floated their crops on rafts down the Ohio and Tennessee rivers to the Mississippi. After selling their crops and the lumber of the raft, the return route was overland on the Natchez Trace. The harbor at Mobile was not large enough to receive trans-Atlantic vessels, so exports had to pass through New Orleans.

People in Tennessee took the Holston river to Knoxville and went westward to Nashville. They traveled to Huntsville, Alabama, where they took the Tuscaloosa Road into the hills of northern Alabama. The Fall Line Road brought people from South Carolina through Columbia, South Carolina, and then connected to the Federal Road. They could also intersect the road at the Saluda Gap in the Blue Ridge of Ashville, North Carolina, along the French Broad river to Knoxville and then to Huntsville. North Carolinians took this route, or they went from Raleigh, North Carolina, to Columbus and Augusta, Georgia, to intersect the Federal Road. New England merchants and craftsmen took the inter-coastal sea route.

The Creek Indians decided to yield to the population expansion from Americans who imposed on them the pressure to leave their homeland in 1830 but decided to remain in Alabama. They were defrauded of their land. They turned to theft and murder but lost their lands. Fifteen thousand were forced to emigrate to the West.

The only German settlement in the state was in Cullman County in 1872. Walter M. Kollmorgan's *The German Settlement in Cullman County, Alabama An Agricultural Island in the Cotton Belt* (Washington, 1941) treats the only German settlement in the state.

Mississippi

The French established the first settlement in Mississippi at Biloxi in 1699 and at Fort Rosalie or Natchez in 1716. Many Tories took refuge there during the Revolutionary War.

By 1729 there were some three hundred French colonists at Fort Rosalie at Natchez.

By 1770 Natchez was filling up with settlers coming overland via the Ohio and Mississippi rivers. Amos Ogden, a navy captain, received a 25,000 acre mandamus 25 miles southwest of the old fort at Natchez. The conditions were that he had ten years to bring one person from other colonies or abroad for every hundred acres. They had to be Protestants. His partners were Richard and Samuel Swayze from New Jersey, to whom he sold 19,000 acres. The Swayze family was part of the Great Puritan migration to Massachusetts, which expanded to Southold, Long Island, New York, before continuing to Chester, New Jersey.

The Swayzes brought their families and neighbors with them to the Natchez in 1772. They named their new home the Jersey Settlement. They organized the first Congregational Church in the state. Anthony Hutchins was another settler who came down the Holston River, the Tennessee River, the Ohio River, and the Mississippi River. He settled along Cole's Creek above Natchez. In addition to the Swayzes, there were the Coleman, Griffing, King, Cory, Luse, Ogden, and Carter families. *The History of the Jersey Settlers of Adams County, Mississippi* (Jackson, Miss.: Hederman Brothers, 1981, 2 vols.) is impressive.

Mississippi was part of British West Florida, which England acquired at the end of the French and Indian War. In 1773, Gen. Phineas Lyman founded the Company of Military

Adventurers, who were veterans of the war. Lyman went to England to claim their bounty land rewards. He returned empty-handed. He did, however, obtain an order-in-council promising provincial officers and soldiers on the same basis as regular troops. Five thousand acres went to field officers and 2,000 acres to captains, subaltern and staff officers. Non-coms received 200, and privates 50 acres. The veterans met at Hartford, Connecticut and sent a delegation to Gov. Chester. They came by sea in 1773 in two groups from Connecticut and Massachusetts. Thaddeus and Phineas Lyman, Moses and Isaac Sheldon, Roger Harmon, and ---- Hancks were from Suffield, Connecticut. Moses Drake, Ruggles Winchell, and Benjamin Barber came from Westfield. Mr. Wolcott was from Windsor, Thomas Comstock and Mr. Weed were from New Hartford. Capt. Silas Crane, Robert Patrick, Ashbel Bowen, John Newcomb, and James Dean were from Lebanon. Abraham Knap was from Norfolk. Nathaniel Hull, James Stoddert, Thaddeus Bradley, and ---- Giles were from Wallingford. William Silkrag, Jonathan Lyon, William Davis, and Hyde were from Strafford or Derby. John Fisk and Elisha Hale were from Wallingford. The second vessel carried West Goodrich from Durham, Hugh White from Middleton, Thomas Lyman and James Lyman, ---- Ellsworth, Ira Whitemore and Sage from Middletown, and Maj. Early from Wethersfield. In the autumn the Massachusetts contingent arrived. James Harmon and his family and Elnathan Smith were from Suffield. William Hurlburt and Elijah Leonard were from Springfield. Sereno and Jonathan Dwight were from Northampton. Joseph Leonard and Josiah Flowers were from Granville, Massachusetts. Harry Dwight and Mrs. Elnathan Smith and her family also came.

Another four hundred families came down the Ohio River in flat boats by way of Boatyard, Sullivan County, Tennessee. By 1802 there were about a hundred survivors who petitioned Congress for confirmation of their old land grant, but nothing was done for them. The Lyman heirs did receive 23,000 acres at a cost of $3,000.

During the Revolutionary War British Governor Chester relaxed the land grant regulations and promised a ten year exemption from quit rents. The colony became a haven for Tories and Loyalists. Large numbers came from Virginia, Georgia, and the Carolinas to Natchez.

In 1798 there were 4,500 people in Mississippi. By 1811 there were 31,306 people–a gain of 27,000. When Mississippi was organized as a territory, its capital was Natchez. In 1817 Alabama was detached from Mississippi.

The Natchez Trace extended from Nashville, Tennessee, to Natchez. A horseman could make the journey in ten days and four hours. In 1803 Congress mandated that the Trace be laid out to a width of 16 feet, but the only improvements were made near Natchez. The route was confined to pack horses; wagon traffic was not possible. The Trace facilitated trade and intercourse with the frontier settlements in the Cumberland River basin. The Indians retained the rights to maintain all ferries and to establish houses of entertainment. People traveled on horseback or on foot. On their return home, settlers had saddle bags of currency. En route they traveled amongst dens of thieves, giving rise to the expression "high way robbery." There was safety in traveling in groups. Jonathan Daniels' *The Devil's Backbone: The Story of the Natchez Trace.* (New York: McGraw Hill, 1962) recounts the road's history,

Southerners lost their markets of agricultural staples. The supply of good land had dwindled, and the soil had worn out due to a century of tobacco planting and primitive farming methods. The Napoleonic Wars brought declining products and widespread distress in the Old

South. Eli Whitney's invention of the cotton gin in 1793 changed society. Optimism was expressed in geographical nomenclature. Mississippi was promoted as the Garden of America.

There was a land boom in 1837 when the last of the Indian lands were opened for purchase.

Following the Civil War, immigrants from Mississippi removed to British Honduras. The ex-Confederates are discussed in Donald C. Simmons' *Dixie by the Carib Sea: Confederate Settlements in British Honduras* (1994) and *Confederate Settlements in British Honduras* (Jefferson, North Carolina: Garland, 2001). They chose to settle there rather than endure Reconstruction.

Louisiana

Louisiana was a part of New France from 1698 to 1762 at which time it was transferred to Spain by the Treaty of Fontainbleu in order to prevent the colony from falling into the hands of the British and for Spain's impending loss of Florida. The Spanish took over effective control in 1769 and held Louisiana until 1800, when it was ceded back to France. The United States acquired it by purchase in 1803.

The first settlers to arrive in Louisiana were the French in 1698. It was France's second major venture in the North America. Earlier in 1608 they had colonized Quebec. As with the English the ratio of men to women made it necessary to send casket girls to the colony. These future brides carried their possessions in a trunk or casket on their backs. They settled on the Red River at Natchitoches. New Orleans was founded in 1718 by Jean Baptiste Le Moyne, Sieur de Bienville. New Orleans became the capital in 1722.

Winston De Ville's *Gulf Coast Colonials: A Compendium of French Families in Early Eighteenth Century Louisiana* (Baltimore: Genealogical Publishing Co., 1968) covers the early French. The Germans are treated in Ellen C. Merrill's *Germans of Louisiana* (Gretna: Pelican Publishing, 2005), Albert J. Robichaux's *German Coast Families: European Origins and Settlement in Colonial Louisiana* (Rayne, La.: Hebert Publications, 1997), and Glenn R. Conrad's *The German Coast, Abstracts the Civil Records of St. Charles and St. John the Baptist Parishes, 1801-1812. (*Lafayette, University of Southwestern Louisiana, 1981*).

A Scotsman, John Law, obtained a concession from the French to introduce German settlers in 1718 and 1719. He publicized his venture in the Rhineland, Wurttemburg, Alsace, Swabia, and Switzerland. Between four and ten thousand responded. They made their way overland to French ports on the Atlantic. Many were stopped en route and threatened with confiscation of their property and loss of their citizenship. Some remained in France and others returned to their homes. Upon arriving at Lorient, they found no provisions and they had to make their own shelter. Cholera broke out and claimed half of them--about 2,000. Four ships sailed in the autumn of 1720. Half of the passengers died in enroute. A hundred and thirty Germans and thirty Swiss actually reached Louisiana. The second ship was captured by pirates at Santo Domingo. Only fifty survived. The fourth ship was not sea worthy and had to return to port. The fifth ship brought three hundred passengers to Biloxi in March 1721. Three more ships arrived in April and May. More than a thousand Germans arrived in eight ships. They settled in St. John the Baptist and St. Charles parishes which became known as the German Coast. In the autumn of 1722 a hurricane felled more of the colonists. Their surnames were modified into French counterparts e.g. Triche, Folse, Himel, and Toups.

John H. Deiler's *The Settlement of the German Coast of Louisiana and the Creoles of*

German Descent (Baltimore: Genealogical Publishing Co., 1969) is about the Germans and Swiss colonists. Helmut Blume and Ellen C. Merrill's *The German Coast during the Colonial Era, 1722-1803: The Evolution of a Distinct Cultural Landscape in the Lower Mississippi Delta during the Colonial Era with Specific Reference to the Development of Louisiana's German Coast* (German Acadian Coast Historical and Genealogical Society, 1990) is also excellent.

Alice D. Forsyth, *German "Pest Ships" 1720-1721* (New Orleans: Genealogical Research Society, 1969) covers the pestilence outbreak among the passengers. John Frederick Nau's *The German People of New Orleans* covers the urban Teutons. (Leiden: E. J. Brill, 1956).

In August 1724 Germans from Frederick County, Maryland, left Hagarstown for Fort Pitt and descended the Mississippi River 14 miles below Baton Rouge. They were Roman Catholics. No preparations had been made to receive the colonists. Those who survived went upriver to the English Turn. Bienville removed Law and gave the colonists grants on the Mississippi River. By 1722 they had four villages and 330 inhabitants. A great hurricane that autumn wrought more destruction. By 1768 they had a 400-man militia force.

With the outbreak of the French and Indian War, the English, who had acquired Acadia in the northeast in 1713 at the end of the War of Spanish Succession, expelled the French. These Acadian families made their way to Louisiana. They numbered five thousand and became known as Cajuns. The sixth volume of Bona Arsenault's *Histoire et Genealogie des Acadiens* (Gretna, La.: Pelican Publishing Company, 1974) is about Louisiana families.

In 1769 Roman Catholic Germans from Hagarstown, Maryland who had gone west by foot to Fort Pitt in Pennsylvania, descended the Ohio and Mississippi rivers. Another group, numbering 57 Roman Catholic Germans and 32 Acadians, came by sea. They could not find the Mississippi River and landed on the coast of Texas, where the Spanish captured them. Eventually they were freed. Their vessel was no longer seaworthy so they went overland to Natchitoches.

"Creole" is a term used to describe someone born in a tropical colony of a European nation. In Louisiana it applies to French, German, Spanish, and black African colonists. It did not apply to the Acadians because they were not born in the tropics. Fearful of losing her possessions in the New World during the war, France secretly ceded Louisiana to the Spanish in 1761. At the peace treaty, Spain gained control of all of Louisiana east of the Mississippi River except New Orleans.

In 1763 the population of Louisiana was seventy-five hundred. Under the Spanish regime that number grew to fifty thousand. The outbreak of King George's War caused the British to expel the French settlers in Acadia. Many of them returned to France or were deported to the English colonies on the Atlantic seaboard. Between five and ten thousand migrated to Louisiana in the Attakapas region and the Acadian coast below Baton Rouge. Immigration to Louisiana was the result of generous policies. Heads of families received 350 to 475 feet of water frontage tracts that extended inland one and one-half miles.

Francisco Bouligny led a group of Spanish colonists to the lower Teche at New Iberia in 1779. In 1779 the Spanish government sought to increase its presence in Louisiana. Settlers from Malaga in southern Spain became established in present-day Iberia Parish. Others came from the Canary Islands during the American Revolution. About two thousand Islenos reached New Orleans. They arrived between 1778 and 1783. Gilbert C. Din's *The Canary Islanders of Louisiana* (Baton Rouge: Louisiana State University, 1988) treats the largest group of Spanish-speaking settlers in Louisiana. About two thousand reached New Orleans in 1778. They settled at

Galveztown and Valenzuela above the city and Sts. Bernard and Barataria below the city. They were Canary Islanders.

Neil J. Toups's *Mississippi Valley Pioneers* (Lafayette La., Nielsen Pub., 1970) covers thirty-seven ship lists of passengers from France to Louisiana between 1718 and 1721.

Refugees from Santo Domingo sought to escape the blood baths on the island and fled to Louisiana in 1791. Among them were the Billeaudeau, du Suia de la Croix, and Daquin families.

British sympathizers settled in Louisiana during the Revolutionary War to avoid the conflict. In 1800 Napoleon forced the Spanish to cede Louisiana to the French.

The Louisiana Purchase in 1803 opened the way for Americans. The next year the southern part of the Purchase was organized as the Territory of Orleans and attracted the most Americans who were drawn by the economic opportunities around New Orleans. Between 1804 and 1806 ten thousand arrived.

Located between the Mississippi and Pearl rivers, Spanish West Florida included Baton Rouge. Americans occupied the area in 1810, and it was incorporated into Louisiana when it became a state in 1812 during the war of that year.

Nicholas Roosevelt's steamboat, *New Orleans,* descended the Ohio from Pittsburgh destined for New Orleans at the mouth of the Mississippi in 1812. Barge traffic had taken three to four months to travel from Louisville, Kentucky, to New Orleans. The steamboat covered the same distance in five or six days.

Many French refugees fleeing war-torn West Indies arrived in New Orleans from May 1809 to January 1810. There were more than ten thousand refugees. Louisiana grew so rapidly that it was admitted to the Union in 1812. During the War of 1812 it was British strategy to divert attention by threatening the east coast of the U.S. in 1814 while at the same time sending their forces in Canada down the Mississippi River. Their naval forces in Jamaica were to secretly make their way into the Gulf of Mexico at New Orleans and thereby conquer the United States in a giant pincer. Fifty ships with 10,000 men sailed for New Orleans before news of the armistice could reach North America. Andrew Jackson had been promoted to a generalship and rushed westward with his Tennessee militia volunteers to confront the British at New Orleans under the command of Sir Edward Pakenham.

Pakenham along with two thousand of his men died at New Orleans on 7 January 1815, unaware that the war was over.

The port of New Orleans was the cheapest destination for nineteenth century European immigration. Passengers could be dislodged at New Orleans and go by river traffic into the heartland of North America; on the return voyage of agricultural and manufactured products shipped downstream.

Earl F. Niehaus's *The Irish in New Orleans 1800-1860.* (Baton Rouge: Louisiana State University, 1969) treats this Roman Catholic exodus.

Bertram Kron's *The Early Jews of New Orleans* (American Jewish Historical Society, 1969) focuses on them. Every Jew who came before 1815 has a biographical sketch. Carol Mills-Nichol, *Louisiana's Jewish Immigrants from the Bas-Rhine, Alsace, France* (Santa Maria, California: Janaway Publishing, 2014),

Milos M. Vuynovich's *Yugoslavs in Louisiana* (Gretna, Louisiana, 1974) traces this Slavic group as does his article "The Dalmatian Yugoslavs in Louisiana" (*Journal of the Louisiana*

Historical Association, VIII, 149-164). John Vidacovich arrived about 1839 from Hercegnovi. By 1850 there were more than 200 and by 1860 about 600 were in Plaquemines Parish. After the Civil War many left New Orleans and went to St. Louis and California.

Ex-Confederates from the Pelican State and from Mississippi immigrated to British Honduras after the Civil War. Donald C. Simonds's *Confederate Settlements in British Honduras* (Jefferson, North Carolina: McFarland, 2001) traces these American exiles.

Chapter Ten: The Trans-Mississippi

United States–Nineteenth Century

After the Congress of Vienna met to deal with the havoc wrought by Napoleon in 1815, five thousand immigrants came to the United States. The treaty allowed inhabitants whose allegiance had been switched to a new government six years to leave without paying a property emigration tax under Article XVII. There was regular ship service available for continental Europeans from Basel, Switzerland, down the Rhine, to Dutch ports from Cologne to Rotterdam. Demobilized soldiers in Great Britain, facing bleak farming prospects, also opted for immigration.

Europe in the nineteenth century experienced a dramatic population increase. There was a tremendous spread of commercial agriculture. The rise of the factory system and inexpensive transportation, notably the steamship and railroads, also contributed to immigration to the United States.

Between 1850 and 1860, the number of Irish immigrants increased from 962,000 to 1,611,000. The Germans increased from 584,000 to 1,276,000; English from 279,000 to 433,500; French from 54,000 to 110,000; Swiss from 13,000 to 53,000; and Scandinavians from 18,000 to 72,599. In the next decade people from the British Isles followed the allure of the discovery of gold in Australia, which was in the British Empire. Accordingly, ships were withdrawn from the Atlantic shipping lanes, causing the price of passage to increase, thereby discouraging immigration to America. In 1855 the outbreak of the Crimean War diverted ships from Atlantic shipping to the Mediterranean to the Crimean battlefields.

The outcome of the Civil War was influenced by geography. The Ohio, the Tennessee, and the Missouri rivers converged on the Mississippi River. Movement of troops and materiel gave the Union the means of winning the war.

The American Civil War ended in defeat for the Confederate States of America. Many of the ex-Confederates were without homes. They did not have a predictable future. Their lives had been disrupted and their careers had been dashed or at least postponed. Between ten thousand and twenty thousand decided to go into voluntary exile and leave their homes and move to Latin America. Others were indicted for treason or war crimes, and they feared they might be sentenced to death. All of them had been disenfranchised. They settled in Canada, Cuba, Brazil, Venezuela, British Honduras, and Mexico. Others went to England, France, Egypt, Japan, Korea, and India. Their destinations were selected by geographical proximity, a common language, and a common culture. The Confederate States of America had commercial ties abroad so British Honduras was one of the earliest new homelands. The Rev. R. Dawson left Mobile, Alabama in 1861 to settle there. Many from Texas joined the exodus to Mexico in 1864. The Emperor Maximilian had given aid to the Confederacy.

Outbreaks of religious intolerance in the Old World was another force that brought 10,000,000 immigrants to America between 1865 and 1890. That number climbed to 15,000,000 between 1890 and 1914.

Iowa

It was not until 1833 that the Fox and Sauk tribes were forced to cede some 9,000 square miles to the United States. Settlers flocked to the new land.

Scandinavians settled in the central and western parts of the state. Holland Dutch occupied the south central area, and the Germans were along the Mississippi River. The Scottish and Welsh located in the southern part, and the Czechs in the east central part. Jim W, Faulkinbury's *The Germans of Iowa and Their Accomplishment* (Iowa City: State Historical Society of Iowa, 1922), Jacob Van Der Zee's *The British in Iowa* (Iowa City: State Historical Society of Iowa) and *The Hollanders of Iowa* (Iowa City: State Historical Society of Iowa, 1912) cover nineteenth-century immigrants.

Missouri

The French were the first Europeans to settle in the future state. They hoped to control the Mississippi River, find the Northwest Passage, and confirm the rumors of wealth in the interior. Marquette and Joliet were the first Europeans to see the Missouri River in 1673. In 1682 LaSalle descended the Mississippi River and claimed the area for France. It was he who named it Louisiana. In 1699 the French established a fur trading station opposite St. Louis–Cahokia. About the same time the Illinois Indians abandoned their homes on the east bank, and moved south along the Illinois River They crossed the Mississippi River, and settled south of St. Louis. The French established Kaskaskia on the left bank of the river and attracted settlers from Canada. It was the center for the fur trade, evangelization, and mineral exploration.

The Illinois country was detached from Canada and assigned to Louisiana for administrative purposes. The French built Fort de Chartres, outside of which the village of Ste. Anne grew up. Colonists came directly from Europe in 1718. In the 1720s, Fort Orleans was established near Brunswick, Missouri. It was abandoned in 1726.

Ste. Genevieve became the first permanent settlement on the west bank of the Mississippi River to help control the trade between Canada and New Orleans. It was also on the approach to the lead mines. By 1745 there were about three hundred people in Missouri. When the best lands around Kaskaskia had been occupied, settlers crossed the river and located on the rich river bottom land on the west bank. By 1751 Ste. Genevieve had eight households and a church.

By the secret treaty of Fontainbleau, France ceded her trans-Mississippi holdings to Spain in 1762. The treaty became public in 1764. The Spanish were keen on attracting settlers and hoped to entice Acadians and Roman Catholic Irish and Germans. They promised a tract of five arpents, tools, and a barrel of maize for a year for every person twelve years of age and older.

St. Louis was established as a fur trading center in 1764 by two New Orleans merchants. The Spanish wanted to check mate the Americans after the Revolutionary War. They lured Roman Catholic priests to the west bank. All of the congregation at Kaskaskia responded. They were upset at the high cost of land in the United States. The passage of the Northwest Ordinance in 1787 forbade slavery above the Ohio River. Many Americans took their slaves and moved to New Spain.

Pierre Louis Lorimer, born of French parents in Louisiana, sought to attract German settlers. He settled the Swiss and Germans on the White River in the Cape Girardeau District. Jacob Neyswanger, John Freiman, Daniel Krentz, Valentine Lorr, and John Probst from North

84

Carolina accepted his invitation. Maj. John Bollinger of Lincoln County, North Carolina brought the first German Protestant preacher. Col. George Mason of Philadelphia, Pennsylvania laid out New Madrid. Americans were the majority of Cape Girardeau settlers. In 1795 the Spanish granted Americans the right to ship their goods through New Orleans.

Moses Austin visited Ste. Genevieve in 1796 because of the nearby lead mines. He settled his family at Potosi in 1798. By 1796, Missouri settlers were American, Spanish, and French. In 1798 Whitewater Creek was settled by Swiss-Germans from North Carolina. By 1840 they had expanded into Wayne County. Daniel Boone settled in St. Charles at the salt licks. Kentuckians located in Perry County, which resembled the barrens of the treeless tract back in Kentucky. Tennesseans were the next most numerous category of Americans who came to Missouri. The Americans initially came to Missouri via the Ohio River Valley. Pennsylvanians, Marylanders, Virginians, and Carolinians followed. The Americans dominated New Madrid, Cape Girardeau, Femme Osage, and Loutre Island. They knew they had to settle away from the rivers where it was healthier and where the land was good. Jackson, Apple Creek, and Perryville were their early settlements.

The Spanish land offices were much closer than those in the United States, and Americans made their decisions to purchase realty because of such.

In 1801 Napoleon forced the King of Spain to return to the French their former holdings in the New World. The next year Americans lost their right to use the port of New Orleans. As Napoleon's situation in Europe became more drastic, he accepted the United States offer to buy Louisiana. There were fewer than ten thousand residents in Missouri. New Madrid was the only English-speaking village. Ste. Genevieve, St. Francois, and St. Louis were French and Spanish speaking.

The Louisiana Purchase in 1803 opened a vast portion of the continent. Fur traders were the first to leave St. Louis in the spring of 1807. The fur trade needed capital to underwrite the expenses and to battle hostile Indians. The Missouri Fur Company was formed in 1809. John Jacob Astor, a German, organized his American Fur Company around a chain of forts from the Great Lakes to the Pacific at the mouth of the Columbia River. The furs would be shipped to the Orient. The War of 1812 brought the lucrative adventure to a close.

The Missouri River, the eighth longest in the world, provided access from St. Louis to the Rocky Mountains. The river is 2,700 miles long. In 1804 the Lewis and Clark expedition set out to explore the West. They returned to St. Louis 23 September 1806. In 1810 Col. Benjamin Cooper blazed the Booneslick trail along the north side of the Missouri River.

In March 1811 the Great Comet was visible in sky. The Russians thought it presaged the invasion of their nation by Napoleon. In the United States it was interpreted as a sign of an impending earthquake. A horde of squirrels pressed south in Indiana a few weeks earlier and plunged into the Ohio river where thousands of their corpses drifted downstream. Charleston, South Carolina had tremors. In October 1811 tremors were reported in Austria, England, and Phillippines. Torrential rains fell in the United States in November. On 16 December 1811 at 2 a.m. there was a weird glow lighting the sky above Missouri. The ground swayed underfoot. It was an earthquake whose center was around New Madrid, Missouri, 140 miles south of St. Louis. The quake was felt over 301,656 miles. An area of 30,000 square miles sank from 5 to 25 feet while other areas were raised as much. The quake created the 18 foot long Realfoot Lake in Tennessee.

The New Madrid earthquake delayed the development of eastern Missouri for a half century. Fissures in the ground were a half-mile long. Trees were bent. The entire cemetery at New Madrid was carried away. Feet of sand covered the land. It caused settlers to travel up the Missouri River in search of a place to locate.

Following the War of 1812, interest in settling in Missouri grew. In October 1819, ten to fifteen thousand settlers crossed the Mississippi at St. Louis. Most headed for Boone's Lick. In 1820 Missouri was admitted as a slave state, but slavery was prohibited above its southern border in any future state's admission. Maine came into the Union as a free state as part of the Missouri Comprise.

Missouri had one of three reserves for bounty lands for those who served in the United States military in the War of 1812. The slave-owning counties were known as Little Dixie. It consisted of the counties of Pike, Ralls, Anderson, Randolph, Callaway, Boone, Howard, and Monroe.

In 1812 the Territory of Missouri was created. There were settlements at St. Louis and St. Genevieve. The Indians owned much of Missouri, so most Americans were somewhat reluctant to venture into the area in search of farms. The Osage ceded their lands in northern Missouri in 1808, and the Quapaw ceded their lands in 1817. All of Missouri was then open for settlement.

Between 1815 and 1819 thirty to fifty wagons filled with those seeking new homes crossed the Mississippi at St. Louis. Farmers from Tennessee occupied the Ozarks because the land there resembled their homes in the Volunteer State. Settlers from Kentucky sought farms along the Missouri River and laid out Booneville and Franklin in 1817. Lexington and Liberty were founded in 1822 and Independence in 1827. The Show-Me-State was the gateway to the West and welcomed the fur traders, the Forty-Niners, and those headed to Oregon, California, and Texas.

The Mexican Revolution of 1820 opened the way for trade with the two thousand people at Santa Fe, New Mexico who were eager to be able to acquire manufactured goods in exchange for furs and silver that Americans sought. The pack horses and wagons set out from Independence, Missouri. By 1824 the trade was well established. In that year eighty men, twenty-five wagons, and one hundred fifty-nine pack horses made the journey with goods valued at $30,000 and returned with furs and silver valued at $190,000. The most important lesson learned by Americans was the use of wagon trains to cross the continent.

The traders discovered the South Pass in the Rockies. They discovered the Snake River route to Oregon, the Humboldt River trail to California, and the Gila River road to the New Southwest. They opened the West to settlers moving westward. Both the Santa Fe and Oregon trails began at Independence.

Following the War of 1812, the government turned its attention to trans-Mississippi exploration. Military outposts kept the Indians in check, encouraged fur traders, and restrained activities by European powers. Fort Smith, Arkansas, and Fort Snelling, Minnesota, were the first two outposts. At Council Bluffs, Iowa, Fort Atkinson was built.

The Platte Purchase added six counties in the northwestern part of the state. The Mormons settled in Missouri in 1831. They were repulsed in 1839.

Robyn and Ken Luebbering's *German Settlement in Missouri: New Land Old Ways* (Columbia: University of Missouri Press, 1996) and *Independent Immigrants: A Settlement of Hanoverian Germans in Western Missouri* (Columbia: University of Missouri Press, 2007) discuss the major immigrant ethnic group in the state.

Arkansas

The settlement of Arkansas was made possible by riparian egress. The Mississippi River formed the eastern border of the state. The White, Arkansas, Ouachita, Red, and St. Francis rivers made inland penetration possible. While the Mississippi River provided the first "road" to Arkansas, its shores were subject to frequent flooding so the settlements grew up along the river. Part of New France from 1673, Arkansas became Spanish in 1762. Arkansas Post was established in 1768. French control was superimposed again in 1800, and the United States acquired possession by virtue of the Louisiana Purchase in 1803.

Federal land was offered at very low prices. The Indian cessions were in 1808 until 1825. The settlers traveled by waterways and settled along them. They used the flatboat, dugout, and keel boat. The flatboat was too unwieldy for poling up the rivers, most of which flowed southeasterly. While the dugout was quite maneuverable, it had a limited capacity for a settler's cargo.

Keel boats combined the features of the other two types of craft. They could be towed or poled upstream. One keel boat could accommodate as many as thirty families. The vessel had a shallow draft, so it could go more places in less water.

Steamboat traffic was introduced in 1820 with the *Eagle,* which ascended the Arkansas from its mouth to Little Rock–a journey of more than a hundred miles. Steamboat service was available on every river in the state by 1840. Steamboat traffic was curtailed due to drought in the 1850s. By the 1870s the railroads had replaced riparian travel.

Settlers moved in the late winter and early spring by water in order to take advantage of the higher water levels and to arrive in time to plant their crops.

Overland travel was on a much smaller scale. There was a military road from Memphis to Indian Territory on Arkansas's western border. It was opened to Little Rock by 1827 and extended to Fort Smith in 1828. In the 1830s a second military road from southern Missouri via Little Rock to Fulton on the Red River was available. Travelers by land did so after they harvested their crops in the autumn.

One of the three federal bounty land reserves for veterans of the War of 1812 was located on the north bank of the Arkansas River. There were some six thousand six hundred grantees. Kathryn Christensen's *Arkansas Military Bounty Grants [War of 1812]* (Hot Springs, Arkansas; Arkansas Ancestors, 1971) gives the patentees' names, warrant numbers, patent dates, and County of location.

A company of men served under Capt. Jesse Bean in the Black Hawk War in 1832. Most of the men were from Independence and Lawrence counties. Others served in the Florida War and Cherokee wars. They came from Conway, Hempstead, Independence, Lawrence, Pope, Pulaski, Randolph, Saline, Sevier, and Washington counties.

In the 1850 federal census Tennesseans accounted for the most people born out of state. Settlers from Tennessee, North Carolina, Kentucky, and Missouri dominated the northern half of the state, while the southern half had more settlers from Alabama and Georgia. More native-born Arkansans lived in Texas than any other state.

After the Civil War, southern Europeans settled between the White and Arkansas rivers. The Poles settled in Pulaski County.

Chapter Eleven: The West

The panic of 1837 prompted Americans to turn their attention to the Great Plains in the west. There was little vegetation. Waterways were lacking. Perpetual winds prevailed. The rivers ran in the wrong direction, except the Missouri, so farmers had no means of getting their produce to market. The lack of trees for building homes, barns, fences, utensils, furniture, and fuel for heating and cooking were serious obstacles. Buffalo chips were the only fuel alternative. The buffalos were a good source of food but were such stupid beasts that they were easily eradicated leaving only rabbits and coyotes.

The one encouraging factor to Great Plains agriculture was that the farmers did not have to clear the land of trees. Annual waterfall was between 10 and 20 inches a year, which caused the rivers to disappear or become a trickle.

Farmers for the first time had to turn to dry farming and using ground water. Settlers were capable of digging wells twenty to thirty feet deep but such wells were not enough. The water level was 500 feet below ground. The settlers solved the problem by drilling wells instead, but they still had the problem of raising the water to the surface. Pumps were required to do so, and the wind mill was the solution.

Texas

Spanish dominion here was based on the explorer, Alvar Nunez Cabeza de Vaca who was in Texas in 1528. The Spanish ignored the area until 1685, when the French claimed it. Texas was too far from Mexico City to encourage settlement north of the Indian infested desert in between. The Spanish sought to win the favor of the Indians and constructed a chain of missions stretching to East Texas in 1690. San Antonio became the first permanent settlement in 1731 when fifty Canary Islanders migrated via Havana and Vera Cruz.

American colonization of Mexico was very much a part of the westward movement from Tennessee. Americans settled west of the Sabine River by 1803, around Nacogdoches. Others crossed the Red River in the north.

Moses Austin, born in Durham, Connecticut, in 1761, moved to Philadelphia in 1783. He began his career smelting lead in Wytheville, Virginia, in 1792. In 1798 he was operating lead mines in Potosi, Missouri. In 1819 he established the Bank of St. Louis, but his bid for prosperity was unsuccessful in his financial pursuits. In order to escape his debts, he opted to relocate in Spanish Texas. He suffered financial setbacks and decided to investigate the possibilities of trading with Mexico. In 1820 he went to Mexico. He informed the Spanish that he wanted to settle on Spanish soil. He represented three hundred other families who wanted to do likewise. He said he was Roman Catholic and had been a Spanish subject in Missouri. He met Baron de Bastrop of San Antonio who intervened on his behalf, the two having met some years ago. Austin became ill en route home and died in June 1821. He asked his son Stephen F. Austin to fulfill his contract.

Stephen Austin left New Orleans to inspect the area for a place suitable for his contemplated colony. He met with the Spanish officials at San Antonio. His agreement was with Spanish governor. It was approved by the Congress of Mexico two years later.

Austin was authorized to introduce three hundred families of proper moral character, and they had to accept the Roman Catholic faith. Each family was to receive a labor (177 acres) and 74 leagues (4,428 acres) for farming and livestock respectively. Austin was to collect 12 ½ cents per acre for his services and a bonus of 65,000 acres when two hundred families were brought into the colony. The land was located in the bottoms of the Brazos, Colorado, and Bernard rivers around San Felipe de Austin. By 1825 there were 2,021 residents. Austin maintained a registry of his families which Villamae Williams abstracted for *Stephen F. Austin Register of Families from the Originals in the General Land Office, Austin, Texas* (St. Louis, Mo.: Ingmire Publications, 1984).

Austin's colony was the first English speaking settlement in Texas. Among his colonists were Zadock and Minerva (Cottle) Woods, who had married in South Woodstock, Vermont, in 1797. Her fifth great-grandfather was William Bradford of Plymouth. She was the first *Mayflower* Pilgrim descendant from New England to migrate to Texas.

The Mexican constitution permitted individual states to authorize colonies headed by an empressario. Back in the United States, federal land was offered for sale at the price of $1.25 an acre. Texas was also more healthy than the Mississippi River Valley, where bilious fever or dysentery and ague or malaria were rampant. By 1824 contracts for two thousand four hundred families had been granted. By 1829 that number had grown to five thousnd four hundred and fifty families.

In 1825 Austin asked the state government for permission to bring three hundred more families. It was increased to five hundred families. A second contract with the state was for one hundred families in 1827, followed by another contract in 1828 for three hundred. Finding families proved difficult because slavery was illegal in Mexico and religiously Americans were overwhelming Protestants. Austin won a concession from the government that Protestants were not required to attend Roman Catholic services. They were denied, however, the right to worship in their own churches.

Austin's colonists came from west of the Alleghenies and south of the Ohio. Missourians were proportionately greater.

Martin de Leon's grant was to bring Mexican families into Texas in 1824. He also enlisted some Irish and some Americans. Victoria was his capital.

Green DeWitt began his colony in 1825. Green DeWitt was to settle four hundred families on the headwaters of the Guadalupe, San Marcos, and Lavaca rivers. They traveled down the Mississippi River to New Orleans and by coastal vessels to the Lavaca River. Most of the colonists were from the Upper South of Alabama, Missouri, Tennessee, and Louisiana, in addition to a family from Pennsylvania. Edward A. Lukes's *De Witt Colony of Texas* (Austin: Jenkins Publishing Co., 1976) covers the counties of Caldwell, De Witt, Fayette, Gonzales, Guadalupe, Jackson, Lavaca, and Victoria.

Hayden Edwards received an empressario grant to settle some eight hundred families near Nacogdoches.

Sterling Clack Robertson founded the largest empressarial colony covering thirty counties in a tract 100 miles long by 200 miles wide.

The Canary Islands are an archipelago off the southwest coast of Morocco. Sixteen families from the islands left for Texas in 1731.

Wavell's colony in extreme northeastern Texas was the least successful. By 1831 there were only one hundred twenty-two families within its boundaries.

James Power and James Hewetson applied for an empressario contract. They agreed to settle Irish and Mexican families. Power recruited three hundred fifty Irishmen from his native Ballygarrett Parish. They landed at New Orleans in 1834. Cholera ravaged the colonists.

Maryland Roman Catholics migrated from Kentucky to Missouri and then located in Lavaca County, Texas, in the 1830s.

In 1834 there were two thousand four hundred Spaniards in Bexar, seven hundred in Goliad, five hundred in Nacogdoches, and thirty in Victoria which Martin de Leon had founded a decade earlier. Between 1821 and 1835 more than thirty-five thousand Americans came to Texas. Many brought their slaves with them. Mexico outlawed slavery in 1829 and in 1830 banned further immigration.

The war of Texas independence in 1836 forced Mexico to recognize the new nation. Santa Anna with two thousand five hundred troops besieged the two hundred Americans at the Alamo in San Antonio. The siege lasted ninety minutes. The deaths of those defenders of the Alamo were avenged at the battle of San Jacinto.

Under the Republic of Texas there were four colonies. The most successful was the Peters Colony in 1841, which covered the counties of Grayson, Collin, Dallas, Ellis, Johnston, Tarrant, Denton, Cooke, Montague, Wise, Parker, Clay, Hood, Erath, Palo Pinto, Wichita, Archer, Baylor, Stephens, Callahan, Shackleford, Throckmorton, Jack, Wilbarger, Eastland, and Young. Most of the 5,386 settlers came from the Ohio River Valley. The famous twin sister cannons were manufactured in Cincinnati, Ohio, and used in the Texas Revolution. Seymour V. Connor did a detailed study in *Peters Colony of Texas: A History and Biographical Sketches of the Early Settlers* (Arrow Curtis Printing, 1974) and *Kentucky Colonization in Texas, A History of the Peters Colony* (Baltimore: Genealogical Publishing Co., 1998.)

The Mercer Colony was founded in 1844. More than twelve hundred settlers were in Collin, Dallas, Ellis, Fannin, Henderson, Hopkins, Hunt, Kaufman, Navarro, Tarrant, and Van Zandt counties.

In 1846 Texas entered the Union as the twenty-eighth state.

The Bettina Colony was a socialistic movement consisting of German scholars from Heidelberg and Giessen in 1847. It was located in Llano County.

There was an Icarian Colony in Denton County established by Etienne Cabot. Most of the inhabitants removed to Nauvoo, Illinois, in the 1850s.

The Mercer Colony of 1844 was another. It extended into Dallas, Ellis, Navarro, Hernderson, Kaufman, Hunt, Hopkins, Collin, and Van Zandt counties. Mormons from Illinois came to Texas to ascertain the possibility of moving there. Lucien Woodward wanted to purchase lands between the Nueces and Rio Grande. The death of Joseph Smith caused the Mormons to decide to go to Utah instead. Lyman Wright insisted that the promised land was Texas and moved some of his fellow believers to Grayson County and then to the area north of Texas on the Colorado River. The Mormons moved to a site on the Perdenales; it was swept away in a flood in 1850.

91

The Adelsverein, an association of German nobility, in March 1844 brought a few thousand German colonists. Thirty-six shiploads of Germans had arrived by 1846. Their settlements were New Braunfels and Fredericksburg.

Gilbert Benjamin, *The Germans in Texas: A Study in Immigration* (Austin: Jenkins Publishing Co., 1974, (Rudolph Biesele, *German Pioneers in Texas* (Austin, n, d.) Chester W. and Ethel H. Geue, *A New Land Beckoned: German Immigrants to Texas 1844-47* (Waco: Texian Press, 1972) treats seven thousand Germans. An additional five thousand are in their *New Homes in a New Land, German Immigration to Texas 1847-61* (Baltimore: Genealogical Publishing Company, 1982). Moritz P. Tilling, *History of the German Element in Texas from 1830 to 1850.* (*Houston,* n. p., 1913) is also valuable.

The Norwegian immigration to Texas was smaller in numbers as described in Axel Arneson, "Norwegian Settlements in Texas," *Southwestern Historical Quarterly,* XLV (1941) 125-35.

There was a colony of Roman Catholic Irish at San Patricio, Texas. Another Irish enclave was in the area of Refugio.

Czechs from Moravia, Bohemia, and parts of Silesia left the port of Hamburg, continued to Liverpool, and then for New Orleans, Louisiana in 1851. They continued to the port of Galveston. These Slavic people settled in Austin, Fayette, Lavaca, and Washington counties. By the time of the Civil War seven hundred had come to Texas. Their number grew to more than fifteen thousand born in the Old World.

The Czechs are covered in a number of works including Robert Janak's *Geographic Origin of Czech Texas* (Hallettsville, Old Homestead Publishing Company, 1985) listing eight hundred and fifty ancestral homes, Edmond H. Heyl's *Villages of Origin, Protestant Czech Immigrants,* V. A. Svreck, *A History of the Czech-Moravian Catholic Communities of Texas.* Edmund H. Heyl's *Villages of Origin (Protestant): Specific Czechs or Moravians, Abstracted from the Register Records of the Ross, Prairie, Wesley, and Brethern Churches, 1872-1900* (Fort Worth: the author, 1983) and Estelle Hudson's *Czech Pioneers of the Southwest* (Dallas: Southwest Press, 1934.)

The Poles established Panna Maria in Karnes County in 1854. They are treated in T. Lindsay Baker's *The First Polish Americans: Silesian Settlements in Texas.* (Lubbock: Texas Tech, 1975), Jacek Przyguda's *Texas Pioneers from Poland: A Study in the Ethnic History* (Los Angeles, 1971), Mieczysilas Haiman's *The Poles in the Early History of Texas* (Annals of the Polish Roman Catholic Union, Archives Museum I: Chicago, 1936) and Edward Dworazk's *The First Polish Colonies of America in Texas, Containing also the General History of the Polish People in Texas* (San Antonio: Naylor Company 1936).

Ukranians are treated in Viktor Balaban and B. Irba's *Ukranintse v Teksasi* (Aalaban, 1976.)

La Reunion was a French socialist colony led by Victor Considerant in Dallas County in 1855. George H. Santerre, *White Cliffs of Dallas, the Story of La Reunion, the Old French Colony* (Dallas: Book Craft, 1955), Margaret F. Hammond's *La Reunion, A French Settlement in Texas.* (Dallas: Royal Publishing, 1958), and Trevia W. Beverly's, *French Heritage in Texas* (Houston: author, 1980) describe the French role.

More than seven thousand Swedes settled in Travis and Williamson counties between 1848 and 1948. The Norwegians settled in Henderson County; many of them moved into Dallas, Van Zandt, Kaufman, and Cherokee counties. The largest settlement of Norwegians was in 1853 in Bosque County. Ole Knutson led the settlers. Ernest Severin, *Svenskarne i Texas ord obild 1838-1918* (Austin: ca. 1919) relates the Swedish history.

Castro's colony was heavily Roman Catholic and attracted 2,134 Alsatians to Medina County. Bobby Weaver's *Castro's Colony, Empressario Development in Texas, 1842-1865* (College Station: Texas A&M University, 1985) and Julia A. Waugh, *Castroville and Henry Castro, Empressario* (San Antonio: Standard Printing Company, 1934) detail the Alsatians.

A colony of Sorbs or Wends led by Jan Killian landed at Galveston and came to Lee County, Texas, in 1854. Their settlement, Serbin, covered 4,254 acres. They spoke a Slavic dialect and were primarily Lutheran. Anne Blasig's, *The Wends of Texas* (San Antonio: University of Texas, 1954), George Engerrrand, *The So-called Wends of Germany and Their Colonies in Texas and in Australia* (San Francisco: R. & E. Research Co., 1972), Lillie (Moerbe) Caldwell, *Texas Wends* (Salado: Anson Jones Press, 1961) cover the Wends from Lusatia in 1854.

Daniel Parker, a Baptist and state senator form Illinois, visited Texas in 1832. He returned home and formed the Pilgrim Predestinarian Regular Baptist Church. The entire congregation moved to Anderson County, Texas, in 1833 from Clark and Crawford counties.

Migration into Texas between 1850 and 1860 was not from the adjacent states of Arkansas and Louisiana. The new settlers leap frogged from Alabama and Tennessee and accounted for half of the population of the state during this decade. The fringe settlers were from Missouri and had previously been in Kentucky. There were large contingents from Georgia and Mississippi. The Georgians located in the piney woods in the northeast along the Red River.

Texas, as the extension of the lower South, seceded from the United States in 1861. With the collapse of the Confederacy, high ranking ex-Confederates as well as those who did not ever want to return to the victorious Union government left the state and immigrated to Brazil as in William C. Griggs, *The Elusive Eden: Frank McMullan's Confederate Colony in Brazil* (Austin: University of Texas Press, 1987). The former Confederates had a large land grant near San Paulo, Brazil. *Vide* Eugene C. Harter, *The Lost Colony of the Confederacy* (Jackson, Miss. University of Mississippi, 1985). Betty Antunes de Oliviera, *North American Immigration to Brazil Tombstone Records of the "Campo" Cemetery Santa Barbara, Sao Paulo, Brazil* (Rio de Janeiro, 1978). Douglas A. Grier did his Ph.D. at the University of Michigan in 1968 and wrote *Confederate Emigrants to Brazil 1865-1870* as his dissertation.

Kansas

In 1821 the Santa Fe Trail traversed the Kansas, and forts, e.g. Fort Leavenworth, were erected along the route to protect settlers.

The Indians were removed from Kansas in 1854, at which time Kansas was opened for settlement. The Kansas-Nebraska Act of 1854 stipulated that residents could decide by vote if Kansas was to be free or slave. Both supporters and opponents of slavery located in Kansas between 1854 and 1861. The era was marked by violence which led to the appellation of "Bleeding Kansas."

Severe famines in Scandinavia caused the Norwegians to settle in Cloud, Clay, Jewell, Brown, Labette, Chautaqua, Greenwood, and Republic counties. The Danes settled in Marshall

County in 1869 and expanded into Cloud, Lincoln, Allen, Philip, Jackson, Hays, and Ellis Counties. In the 1860s the Swedes made their way to Smoky Hill, Neosho, Republican, and Blue Valley. Another colony of Swedes settled at Manadahl in Pottawatomie County in 1860, having sojourned in Illinois a decade earlier.

Bohemians selected Marshall County between 1861 and 1877. Other Bohemians from Michigan joined them.

French from Canada as well as from France and Belgium came to Kansas after the Civil War.

Swedes settled at Stolter, in Logan County in the 1870s and 1880s. Some of them had previously been in Princeton, Illinois. Among their surnames were Lagergren, Anderson, Johnson, Fagerstrom, Hogberg, Ogren, Folson, Berman, Ericson, Eastburg, Melgren, Sutherland, Lunstadt, Christensen, and Olson.

Germans from Russia settled in Ellis, Russell, and Rush counties.

A settlement of Quakers was near Baxter Springs, and a second colony from Indiana came to Rice County.

Dunkards from Maryland came to Dickinson County.

The Mormons arrived in Stafford County in 1875.

Mennonites came to Marion County. They arrived in the 1870s and called their settlement Gnadenau.

Irish Catholics settled at Atwood and Tully.

Slightly more than seventeen thousand Black Americans were in Kansas by 1870. They were from Tennessee, Texas, Louisiana, and Mississippi. They were the first general migration of Blacks after the Civil War. They were fleeing the South, where the Ku Klux Klan were harassing them. The Kansas of John Brown was their one sure promised land. Their numbers grew to 43,107 in 1880, 49,710 in 1890, and 52,003 in 1900. Cherokee County was one of their largest settlements. Historical background of Blacks in Kansas in the nineteenth century include Nell Irvin Painter's *Exodusters: Black Migration to Kansas after Reconstruction* (Regents Press of Kansas, 1978) and Robert G. Athearn's *In Search of Canaan: Black Migration to Kansas 1879-1880* (New York: Knopf, 1977).

South Carolinians migrated to Pottawatomie County. Kentuckians were in Cowley County in 1869; Tennesseans in 1872 to Abilene; Massachusetts Yankees arrived in 1873 in Edwards County. Settlers from Bridgeport, Connecticut, arrived at Smoky Hill. More Nutmeggers from New Haven settled at Osborne and Smith counties. New Yorkers settled in Big Blue in 1870.

Twenty thousand Kansans served in the Union forces in the Civil War. They suffered the highest mortality rate in the Union.

Nebraska
Stragglers from the Gold Rush in California, the Mormon migration, and the Oregon migration were some of the earliest settlers. Some of them returned from their westward trek when they saw the Rocky Mountains. In the 1850s, Germans located in Nebraska. Germans from Russia arrived in the 1870s. The latter settled in Lancaster County and its environs.

The Czechs or Bohemians are treated in Rose A. Rosicky's *A History of Czechs (Bohemians) in Nebraska* (Omaha: Czech Historical Society of Nebraska, 1929) and Margie

Sobotka, *Nebraska-Kansas Czech Settlers, 1891-1895* (Omaha: Czech Historical Society of Nebraska, 1929).

Oklahoma

The United States acquired Oklahoma in the Louisiana Purchase in 1803. It was attached to Missouri Territory in 1812. Indian Nations were being sent there in 1817 from Alabama, Georgia, and Florida. They were the Creek, Cherokee, Chickasaw, Choctaw, and Seminole. It was designated Indian Territory in 1839. During the Civil War the Five Nations sided with the Confederate States of America. About three thousand Indians supported the Confederacy. Railroads crossed the area in the 1870s.

Private ownership of federal lands was by means of Land Runs. The first was in 1889 and attracted fifty thousand people. Farmers from Illinois, Iowa, and Kansas settled in the western and northwestern part Oklahoma. The southern and eastern part drew settlers from Arkansas, Missouri, and Texas. The 1893 land run drew nearly a hundred thousand settlers. The oil boom at Bartlesville brought thousands more to the Twin Territories. Cattlemen moved from Texas.

In 1817 the Oklahoma was subdivided among the five Indian nations, Creek, Cherokee, Chickasaw, Choctaw, and Seminole. By 1872 railroads were bringing settlers. Congress yielded to pressure and purchased the Unassigned Lands and No Man's Land from the Indians in 1889. Land runs became the method of allocating lands on a given date on a first-come basis in the western and northwestern parts of the state. The southern and eastern parts of the state attracted farmers from Arkansas, Texas, and Missouri.

Vide An Index to the 1890 United States Census of Union Veterans and Their Widows in Oklahoma and Indian Territories; also an Index to Records from the Oklahoma Union Soldiers Home (Oklahoma City; Oklahoma Genealogical Society, 1970).

A second land run was in 1893. It attracted nearly one hundred thousand new settlers.
Two good sources on the Germans in Oklahoma are Robert C. Rohrs's *The Germans in Oklahoma* (Norman: University of Oklahoma Press, 1980) and Douglas Hale, *The Germans from Russia in Oklahoma.* (Norman: University of Oklahoma Press, 1980).

Utah

Joseph Smith, a Vermonter, was the founder of Mormonism. His father moved the family to Palymra, New York, in 1816. They relocated in Kirtland, Ohio, where they aroused strong local opposition. After sojourning in Missouri the Mormons relocated in Nauvoo, Illinois. They were joined by nearly five thousand British Mormons.

Brigham Young led the Mormons to Nauvoo, Illinois, where there were twelve thousand in 1840. The great exodus to the Great Salt Lake, in what was Mexico at the time, occured in 1847. They drove thirty thousand head of cattle with them. In 1846 the Mormons formed the only faith-based regiment in American military history for service in the Mexican War. It was the fifth regiment.

Mormon settlers arrived in Utah 24 July 1847 under the leadership of Brigham Young. By 1850 the settlers numbered 11,380.

In 1849 the Mormons created the state of Deseret. It included parts of California, Oregon, Idaho, Wyoming, Arizona, and New Mexico as well as Utah.

Their missionary activities were especially successful in Great Britain where their number grew to fifty thousand by 1868. The English Mormons also came to Zion, leaving the United Kingdom via the port of Liverpool for the North American Atlantic seaboard. By river, canal, and railroad they made their way to the Mormon Trail. Between 1850 and 1900 more than ninety thousand Mormons from abroad arrived in Utah, including converts from German and Scandinavia as well as Great Britain. Wallace Earl Stegner's *The Gathering of Zion*: *The Story of the Mormon Trail* (New York: McGraw-Hill, 1962) is the history of that roadway.

The Mormon colonization of successive arable valleys served to disperse them throughout Utah. They founded a hundred new towns within their first decade in the West. Between 1856 and 1860 some eight thousand immigrants came in handcart companies. The first transcontinental railroad was completed in 1869 at Promontory Point.

The opposition to the Mormons due to the practice of polygamy prompted many Mormons to flee to Sonora and Chihuahua, Mexico, and to Alberta, Canada. The practice was discontinued in 1890.

Utah was half-way between Missouri and California and contributed to the settlement of the Pacific states. The Mormons made the first roads, first bridges, and first communities. A third of the settlers of California and Oregon from 1849 followed the Mormon Trail. They opened up southern Iowa, the Missouri frontier, Nebraska, and Wyoming.

Between 1847 and 1868 there were nearly fifty thousand converts from Great Britain, Germany, and Scandinavia.

The Mormon Trail was different than many other trails in the trans-Mississippi area because travel was in both directions. The greatest single influence in the settlement of the west was the railroad. In fact, it would have been impossible to settle the West without the railroad. The railroads replaced cattlemen with farmers. The first railroad boom ended with the panic of 1857. Railroad construction revived after the Civil War. The depression of 1873 ended the post bellum prosperity, but it was followed by the largest boom between 1878 and 1888.

The best prospects for a transcontinental railway was the central route across the West. It was the shortest, had the fewest obstacles, and served the largest population. The Pony Express, the telegraph, and post Civil War prosperity favored the trans-continental railroad in 1869 when the Union Pacific met the Central Pacific, and large scale mining. The choice of the name Union was in deference to the Union soldiers in the Civil War.

Circa 1895 Italians and Slavs arrived in Utah via rail. The Greeks joined them in 1903.

New Mexico

San Juan was the first settlement in New Mexico in 1598. About 1610 Santa Fe became the capital. The indigenous Indians opposed the Spanish colonists for centuries and were especially fierce around 1680. They captured Santa Fe forcing the Spanish to retreat to El Paso. The Spanish regained control in 1692-93 and recruited families from Mexico City to go to Santa Fe. Albuquerque was founded in 1706.

Angelico Chavez's *Origins of New Mexico Families in the Spanish Colonial Period* (Santa Fe Museum of New Mexico Press, 1992), David H. Snow's *New Mexico's First Colonists; the 1597-1600 Enlistments for New Mexico under Juande Onate, Adelante & Gobernador* (Hispanic

Genealogical Research Center, New Mexico, 1998), and Jose Antonio Esquibel's *The Spanish Recolonization of New Mexico: An Account of the Families Recruited at Mexico City in 1693* (University of New Mexico Press, 1998) treat the Spanish colonists. The King's Highway is the subject of Christine Preston's *The Royal Road: El Camino Real from Mexico City to Santa Fe* (University of New Mexico Press, 1998).

The Santa Fe trail opened in 1821, resulting in much commerce with the United States. It was 780 miles long and extended from Independence, Missouri, to Santa Fe. It continued another thousand miles through El Paso to Chihuahua and Durango, Mexico. Residents of Santa Fe bought goods brought from the port of Vera Cruz. The Apache harried them the last five hundred miles.

Initially the goods were carried by pack horses. Wagon caravans avoided rivers and traveled in parallel columns for safety. Three or four teams of oxen pulled each wagon. There was a high death rate of the beasts because there was no forage for them along the trail. The migrants could quickly form a circular corral with the livestock in the center for safety. The wagon trains left in May and arrived in Santa Fe in July. The goods they carried commanded prices ten to twenty times more than in St. Louis. The traders made their return journey laden in gold and furs. Indian depredations were so widespread that soldiers accompanied each caravan.

Gen. Stephen Kearney occupied New Mexico in the Mexican War. The Gadsden Purchase added the counties of Catron and Grant in the Gila Valley.

Arizona

The first permanent settlement was at Tucson in 1776. Spanish colonists from the Mexican states of Sonora and Sinalo settled in the Gila Valley. Arizona north of the Gila River became part of the United States after the Mexican War. The rest of the state was part of the Gadsen Purchase. Mormons moved into the area in the 1850s.

Nevada

The United States acquired Nevada by the Treaty of Guadalupe Hidalgo in 1848 following the Mexican War. Nevada was one part of the United States from which fortune hunters made their way west to the Gold Rush in California in 1849. In Nevada the lure was not gold but silver. Unlike the mining in California, in Nevada it was done in deep underground mines. Most of the miners were immigrants in the boom period of the 1860s and 1870s. The rush began at Virginia City with the Comstock Lode in 1859.

The Mormons established Mormon Station in 1851. Later it was renamed Genoa Lake. By 1855 they had a chain of colonies from eastern to southern Nevada. In 1861 Nevada became a territory. *Vide* Adam S. Eterovich's *Gold Rush Pioneers from Croatia, Bosnia-Hercegovina and the Boka Kotor* (San Carlos, Calif.: Ragusan Press, 1995). It covers settlers from the Balkans as does his *Yugoslavs in Nevada, 1859-1900 Croatians/Dalamatians, Montenegrins, Hercegovinians* (San Francisco, California: R & E Research Associates,1973). Nevada had a population of 20,000, which was one-sixth of the population required for statehood.

The Chinese and Hindus laid the rails in Nevada. The Italians and the Swiss burned charcoal for the mine smelters and raised dairy herds. The Cornish and Irish worked the mines, and the French Canadians were the lumberjacks around Lake Tahoe. The Germans tended to settle in the fertile valleys and produce food stuffs. The Slavs and Greeks worked in the mine smelters in eastern Nevada. The Basques and Scots were the sheep herders. Most Nevadans prized their ownership of personal property but most had no realty.

Typical of migrants were the Clemens brothers–Samuel and Orson. In 1861 they made their way to Nevada by overland journey via steamboat and stagecoach. They brought with them a Colt revolver, a Smith & Wesson seven shooter, blankets, pipes and tobacco, silver coins, some U.S. Statutes, and Webster's *Abridged Dictionary*. Their baggage weighed a thousand pounds.

Colorado

Interest in Colorado exploded with the Pikes Peaks gold rush in 1858. More than fifty thousand were attracted. The communities of Boulder, Denver, Gollden, and Pueblo were established as supply bases. The removal of the Ute Indians to reservations in Utah in 1881 opened up the western part of the state. The cooler dry air was believed to be a cure for tuberculosis, so that by 1900 one-third of the residents of the state had come to treat the disease.

North Dakota

North Dakota was formed from the Louisiana Purchase and (the southeast half) from former British territory.

Scots from Canada established the first permanent settlement at Pembina in 1812. Even though the government offered free land, the Civil War and the Indian wars discouraged settlement. With the coming of the railroads in 1872, the Norwegians were the most numerous settlers. Large numbers of Swedes, Danes, Icelanders, Czechs, Poles and Dutch also came. From Canada came the French. The Germans settled around Bismarck and the south central counties, where they called their settlements Leipzig, Strassburg, and Danzig. Cynthia Anne Frank Stupnik's *Steppes to Neu Odessa* (Bowie, Maryland: Heritage Books, 2002) discuses these settleents. The discovery of gold in 1875 in the Black Hills and the coming of the railroads from 1878 to 1888 stimulated the land boom.

Vide also *Pioneer History: Minnehaha County's Norwegian Pioneers: History from the Year 1866 to 1893* (Sioux Falls, n.p., 1976) and *History of the Finnish Settlers in Brown and Dicky Counties of South and North Dakota, 1881-1955.*

South Dakota

French explorers visited the area in 1742 but lost their claims following the French and Indian War in 1763. The United States acquired the area in 1803 in the Louisiana Purchase. The next year Lewis and Clark led their expedition of the West. Fur traders were the only visitors before 1858, when the Yankton Sioux ceded their claim to the United States. Dakota was set up as a vast territory in 1861. About 200 men served in the Union Army. Montana was split off in 1864 and Wyoming in 1868. Dakota Territory was subdivided in 1867. The discovery of gold in the Black Hills in 1875 drew many settlers. The coming of the railroads led to more settlers in 1878-1888. South Dakota entered the union in 1889.

Wyoming

The era of the mountain men spanned two decades from 1820 to 1840. Unlike the Missouri river fur trapping where Indians did the trapping, whites did so in Wyoming. Laramie was the first permanent settlement in 1834. It was a supply depot on the Oregon Trail with nearly fifty thousand going through the fort in 1849. Fort Bridger was settled in 1842. Between 1841 and 1868, Wyoming bore the brunt of the westward migration along the route from Fort Kearney to Fort Laramie. Between three hundred and fifty thousand and four hundred thousand migrants arrived. The 1859 gold rush at Pikes Peak drew the migrants across Wyoming. Pony Express stations were eight to twenty miles apart.

The removal of the Arapaho and Cheyenne to reservations and the defeat of the Sioux in 1877 opened up northern Wyoming for cattle grazing.

Montana
By the time of the Centenary of the nation, there was a tremendous boom in the cattle industry, notaly in Montana. The expanding industrialization and urbanization increased the demand for foodstuffs. In fact, the acreage devoted to the cattle industry in the nation surpassed that of cultivation. Railroads linked the West to the markets in the East. The federal government had a generous land use policy. The holdings of the Indians and the slaughter of the buffalo left the grazing ground free for occupation.

Idaho
The Lewis and Clark expedition visited Idaho in 1805. Fur traders built a trading post in 1835 on the Snake River. The Oregon Trail traversed the state. Mormons from northern Europe founded Franklin in 1860. A mining boom occurred between 1860 and 1863. The Indians were a barrier to settlement until the 1880s when they were placed on reservations. In the 1880s there was a second mining boom. Idaho's 40 mile northern border with Canada is the shortest in the nation.

Chapter Twelve: The Pacific Coast

It is one of the curiosities of Anglo settlement that the Pacific Coast was settled, by and large, before the Mountain States to their east. The primary reason for this hop-over phenomenon is climate and topography. The harsh winters and lack of rainfall discouraged conventional farming until after the Civil War–even in the western Plains states. As I outline below, the Pacific Coast had already been settled for military purposes, in the case of Spanish California, or by fur traders, in the British instance. The discovery of gold in California brought thousands of miners and statehood almost overnight, while wagon trains of farming families destined for the Willamette Valley and other rich terrain of Oregon and Washington populated the rest of the coastline. Favorable land policies on the part of the U.S. and territorial governments also fueled this in migration. California achieved statehood in 1850, scarcely a year or so after gold was discovered. Oregon became a state in 1859, and Washington did so some 30 years later.

Oregon
In 1792 both the Americans and the English sailed up the Columbia River and laid claim to the area. Their rivalry lasted until 1846.

The fur trade was the factor that drew them. Missionaries entered the area in the 1830s. The first migration was in 1839 under the leadership of T. J. Farnham. More migrations followed in 1842 when over a hundred persons were piloted by Elijah White. In 1843 Dr. Marcus Whitman led a thousand settlers to Oregon. In 1845 they left Westport and Independence, Missouri. It was not until 1846 that the two nations fixed their common border at the 49th parallel. The Donation Land Act of 1850 gave every male over 18 years of age who was already in Oregon 320 acres. If he married by 1 December 1851, his wife could have an additional 320 acres. Males who settled in Oregon by 1853 received 160 acres. If a man had a wife, his total acreage was 320. Oregon's population doubled in the next decade. The completion of the Union Pacific Railroad in 1869 was a significant factor in the redoubling of the population within the next thirty years.

Washington
John Jacob Astor established Astoria as a trading post in 1812. The missionary Marcus Whitman began the second settlement at Walla Walla in 1836. The Willamette and Columbia valleys were the most preferred settlement sites. Americans from the Ohio, Mississippi, and Missouri river valleys opted to forego the unsettled regions of Texas and California over the broad Willamette Valley. The boundary with British Canada was accepted in 1846. Gold was discovered near Walla Walla in 1856.

California
The first to establish settlements in California were the Spanish. They settled San Diego in 1769 and Monterey in 1770. They set up a chain of Franciscan missions for both religious and economic reasons. They also served to forestall the Russians. The Spanish ranches were vast domains. The Russians are documented in James R. Gibson and Alexei A. Istomin's *Russian California, 1806-1860; a History in Documents* (London , Hakluyt Society, 3rd Series, vols. 26 &

27, 2014.)

John August Sutter set up the Kingdom of New Helvetia in the Sacramento River Valley in 1839. He was from Switzerland, as reflected in his choice of the Latin name for his settlement. Americans occupied California in the Mexican War. California was ceded to the United States in 1848, nine days before gold was discovered at Sutter's mill. People from all over the United States as well as Asia, Australia, and Europe flocked to the state. More than one hundred thousand came. In 1849 upwards of seven hundred ships brought an estimated forty thousand people.

In 1846 the Spanish/Mexican population numbered fewer than eight thousand people.

The gold rush led to a jump of more than a thousand miles between the United States settlements in the east and California. By 1850 there were 115,000 inhabitants.

Some Forty-Niners took the sea route around the Cape Horn or across Panama to San Francisco. The trip on clipper ships took about ninety days around Cape Horn. The completion of the railroad across the Isthmus reduced the forty-eight mile journey to three weeks or less. The water route took much less time than the overland routes, and it did take prospectors directly to the gold fields.

During the Civil War the southern mail route linking the Union with California was vulnerable to Confederate attacks. The United States was eager to maintain ties with gold rich California and silver-rich Nevada.

Thousands of Chinese laborers came to construct the transcontinental railroad which was completed in 1869. The railroads vied with each other, and a rate war and a real estate boom in 1869 led to another wave of immigrants.

Marie Northrop's *Spanish Mexican Families of Early California* 1769-1850 is devoted to the Hispanic settlers. (New Orleans: Polyanthos, 1976, 2 vols.)

California's ethnic groups are treated in Miecislaus Haiman's *Polish Pioneers of California* (Chicago: Polish R. C. Union of America, 1940); Meier Vjekoslav's *The Slavonic Pioneers of California* (San Francisco: R. & E. Research Associates, 1968); Maurice E. Perret's *Les colonies tessinoises en California* (Lusanne: F. Rouge, 1950), covers the Italian Swiss; Jacek Przygoda, *Polish-Americans in California, 1827-1977* (*Los Angeles: Polish American Historical Society, 1978*), covers the Poles; Jack B. Coldham's *History of Pioneer Jews in California* (R&E Research Associates, 1971) covers the Jews from 1849-1870; and Thomas O. Stine's *Scandinavians on the Pacific: Danish, Swedish, Norwegian* (R.& E. Research Associates, 1968) covers the north Europeans.

Chapter Thirteen: Alaska, Hawaii, and Canadian Settlements

The purpose of this final, somewhat miscellaneous, chapter is twofold in nature. In the first instance, I have added a few comments about European contact with Alaska and Hawaii, our 49th and 50th states. Since neither state was established as an American territory until after the Civil War, each one is outside the focus of this work. Even so, readers may be interested in some of the milestones and references for additional research I have noted.

The majority of the chapter concerns settlement of the Canadian provinces Quebec, Nova Scotia, and Ontario. During the colonial and Early National period of American history, these provinces were not only Canada's most populated but also possessed histories that overlapped with our own. For example, Nova Scotia was both a destination for Scottish and Irish immigrants and a stopover for people whose ultimate destination was New England. For its part, Ontario's population was greatly increased by the arrival of Loyalist Americans who fled the United States during and after the Revolutionary War in order to remain under British rule. Finally, many Americans who reside in one of the states that borders these three provinces today is likely to possess a genealogical connection to families on the Canadian side.

Alaska

The first permanent white settlement in Alaska was at Kodiak Island by the Russians in 1784. Americans and British involved in the fur trade arrived shortly thereafter. The Russians established their first settlement in 1804 in Sitka.

The fur of the sea otter was in 5 foot long pelts which were highly valued by the Chinese and led to the first settlements. Russians in Alaska numbered between five hundred and eight hundred. Defeated in the Crimean War, Russia had to withdraw from Alaska. Russia sold Alaska to the United States in 1867.

Between 1851 and 1880 ice shipments to California for the preservation of food stuffs was an important factor until ice making machines replaced the floating ice blocks. The first real gold strike was at Juneau in 1880 The capital was named for Joseph Juneau. Hundreds of thousands poured into Alaska in 1896 when the Klondike Gold Strike occurred. Twenty thousand flocked to Nome in the rushes of 1899 and 1900.

Hawaii

Capt. James Cook visited the islands in 1778 in his quest for a passage to Asia. New England missionaries arrived in 1820. During the next decade, laborers and settlers began arriving. Mrs. Robert G. Rigler's *Descendants of New England Missionaries to the Sandwich Islands (Hawaiian Islands) 1820-1900* (Honolulu: the author, 1984) is based on genealogical data from the Hawaiian Mission Children's Society.

Quebec

Champlain led the earliest French colonists to Quebec between 1608 and 1635. The first family were the Heberts, who arrived in 1617. The colonists came from the northwestern French provinces of Brittany, Maine, Perche, Picardy, Ile de France, and Normandy. They included the families of Amiot, Boucher, Bourdon, Cloutier, Cote, Couillard, Delaunay, Deportes, Giffard, Guyon, Juchereau, Langlois, Marsolet, Martin, Nicoles, and Pinquet. Between 1665 and 1673 the French sent approximately eight hundred young women to Quebec as brides. They were known as the King's Daughters. France lost Quebec to the British at the end of the of the French and Indian War in 1763. The population was about ten thousand inhabitants.

The forty-seven volume set, *Repertoire des actes de bapteme, marriage, sepulture et des rescensements du Quebec ancien.* (Montreal: University of Montreal, 1980) is a massive compilation based on church and civil data. Jean-Pierre Wilhelm's *German Mercenaries in Canada* (Bedoeil, Quebec: Maison ds mots (1985). The Huguenots in Quebec are treated in Robert Larin's *Breve histoire des Protestants en Nouvelle-France et au Quebec, XVe-XIXe* siecles (Saint-Alphones-de-Granby, 1998). Linda Corup's *Index* to *the Loyalists of the Eastern Townships of Quebec* (Bolton, Ont., the author, 2003) is quite useful.

Nova Scotia

The French from the area around LaRochelle settled in Acadia. In 1613 Port Royal was sacked by the Virginians led by Samuel Argyall. In 1621 Sir William Alexander sought to create a Scottish settlement. Halifax, Nova Scotia was settled in 1749. The English settlers, however, soon began removing to older settlements. John Dick, a Scottish merchant, was assigned the task to recruit new settlers. They came from the Rhineland Pfalz, Baden, Wurttemberg, Hesse Darmstadt, Switzerland and Montebeliard. The British promised free transportation, a year's supply of food, tools, implements, and some building materials. In return the settlers were expected to labor at building roads and forts. Dick shipped about two thousand seven hundred people between 1750 and 1752, of whom more than four hundred were drawn from Montebeliard who spoke French. They were known as the "Foreign Protestants." Some of them later settled along the Northwest Ranges and St. Margaret's Bay southwest of Halifax. In 1771 some of them settled at Lunenburg. Among them were the Boutellier, Dauphinee, Coulton, Jolimois (Jollimore), Grosrenaud (Grono), Tetteray, Langille, Joudry, and Petrequin families.

The Loreillard family arrived on the *Beaufort*. They had their origins in Porrentury, Switzerland.

In 1755 British troops expelled approximately six thousand Acadians to France, England, Louisiana, and other English colonies. In 1758 Charles Lawrence, Governor of Nova Scotia, sought to attract colonists form New England. Over the next few decades more than eight thousand from Rhode Island, eastern Connecticut, eastern Massachusetts, and southeastern New Hampshire arrived.

The Jacquin and Malbon families relocated in Maine; the Calame and Duvoisin families removed to Pennsylvania; and the Vuilamets went to New York.

Following the Highland clearances in Scotland, the Rev. Norman McLeod led his congregation to Nova Scotia. They sailed on the *Hector* in September 1773.

John Dick, a Scottish merchant, recruited foreign Protestants between 1750 and 1752. About two thousand five hundred responded. One-sixth were Montbeliard. The Jacquin and Malbon families settled in Maine, the Calame and Duvoisin went to Pennsylvania, and the Coulon and Vuilamet to New York. Later the (Jean) Perrin family went to Ohio.

104

The Irish from 1761 to 1863 and the Scots from the 1770s to 1870 in Atlantic Canada are treated in Terrence M. Punch, *Erin's Sons: Irish Arrivals in Atlantic Canada,* (Baltimore: Genealogical Publishing Co., 2009, 4 volumes), and *Some Early Scots in Maritime Canada* (Baltimore: Genealogical Publishing Company, 2011-2012. 3 volumes.) Many of the Irish later settled in the United States.

Michael H. Marunchak, *The Ukrainian Canadians*: A *History* (Winnipeg; Ukranian Free Academy of Sciences, 1970) relates the role of the Ukrainians.

Several dozen Hessian auxiliary troops remained in Nova Scotia in the vicinity of Annapolis. Two thousand military settlers are identified in Virginia Easley DeMarce, *German Military Settlers in Canada after the American Revolution* (Arlington, Va: author, 1984). American Loyalists came in 1783 and later. Some of them were Germans. Black Loyalists settled at Birchtown near Guyborough and in the Preston-Cherry Brook district outside Dartmouth.

Clifford Neal Smith, *Whereabouts of Some American Refugees 1784-1800*: *The Nova Scotia Land Grants* (McNeal: Wheatland Publications, 1992-1995) aids in their geographical location. Nova Scotia had a population of 20,000 at the end of the American Revolutionary War. They were overwhelmed with the arrival of 4,000 Loyalists. The province of New Brunswick was created to cope with them. Among them were the Black Loyalists, who sailed from New York City in 1783. Previously they had lived in South Carolina, Georgia, and Florida. Ruth Holmes Whitehead, *Black Loyalists: Southern Settlers of Nova Scotia's First Free Black Communities* (Halifax: Nimbus Publishing, 2013) and Graham R. Hodges, *The Black Loyalist Directory: African Americans in Exile after the American Revolution* (New York: Garland Publishing, 1996). James W. St. G. Walker, *The Black Loyalists: The Search for a Promised Land in Nova Scotia and Sierra Leone, 1783-1876* (New York: Africana Publishing Co., 1976). In 1791, fifteen ships transported many of the Black Loyalists to Freetown, Sierra Leone, in West Africa.

Heinz Lehman's *The German Canadians* (St. John's, Newfoundland: Jesperson, 1986) treats them.

The Jews who had come from England to Rhode Island came to Halifax in 1751. *Vide* Benjamin G. Sack's *History of the Jews in Canada* (Montreal: Harvest House, 1965.)

Winthrop P. Bell's *The Foreign Protestants and the Settlement of Nova Scotia, the History of a Piece of Arrested British Colonial Policy in the Eighteenth Century* (Halifax: Nimbus Publishing, 2015) pertains to the Huguenots. Michael A. Harrison's *Canada's Huguenot Heritage, 1685-1985* does likewise (Huguenot Society of Canada, 1987). More than 1,400 Huguenots came to Canada..

Ontario

With the outbreak of the American Revolution, a few families from Massachusetts and the Mohawk Valley in New York sought refuge in Ontario. One thousand left Boston in March 1776. Ten thousand Loyalists came to Ontario. They settled along the Bay of Quinet in 1782. The next year more Loyalists arrived and founded Kingston. From 1786 to 1803, the high cost of land in Pennsylvania prompted more German families from Franklin, Lancaster, Montgomery, and Bucks counties to relocate in Ontario.

In 1789 Sir Guy Carleton, Lord Dorchester, Governor-General of Canada proposed to put a mark of honor on the Loyalists who joined the Royal standard before 1783. They were authorized to used the designation United Empire Loyalist.

From 1792 to 1796, the colonial governor, John Graves Simcoe, encouraged Germans in other colonies who had supported King George III to relocate in Ontario. They were able to acquire cheaper lands and to avoid military service. He also attracted Germans from Hamburg who had first settled in the Genesse Valley of New York in 1794. Even though he offered them 200 acres in York County, they were not farmers and moved elsewhere. Following the Napoleonic Wars, the fall in commodity prices, and crop failures prompted settlers to come. Richard E. Vance, *Imperial Immigrants: Scottish Settlers in the Upper Ottawa Valley, 1815-1840* (Dundurn: Toronto Ontario, 2012). In 1824 Amish Mennonites from Germany took up 60,000 acres. A group from Electoral Hessen arrived in 1824.

Quakers from Dutchess County, New York had not supported the Revolutionary War and lost their property in the United States. They migrated to Ontario between 1784 and 1812. They founded Adolphustown. They were also from Bucks County, Pennsylvania and Burlington County, New Jersey. Among them were the Doane, Hollingshead, Rogers, and Haines families.

Scots from Tryon County, New York came to Glengarry, Stormont, and Dundas in 1784. They were later joined by soldiers from the disbanded Highland Regiment, the Glengarry Fencibles. In the aftermath of the Napoleonic Wars falling commodity prices, discharged soldiers, and adverse weather conditions in Europe led to immigration.

Twenty-six thousand Irish from County Cork came to Ontario. The first contingent arrived in 1823. A second group numbered two thousand and twenty-four.

John Mathews, who was born in Glamorganshire, Wales, acquired 1,800 acres in the Talbot Settlement in Middlesex County.

In 1847 more than one hundred four thousand immigrants escaped the Irish Potato Famine and migrated to Canada. Many arrived quite ill, suffering from typhus.

About the Author

Lloyd deWitt Bockstruck was born 26 May 1945 in Vandalia, Illinois–the western terminus of the National Road. He was awarded an Honor Scholarship to Greenville College in 1963 for ranking in the top ten per cent of his secondary school class. He received his bachelor of arts *cum laude* with double majors in biology and history/political science and a minor in psychology/education in 1967. He received a graduate teaching assistantship in the Department of History at Southern Illinois University and earned his Master of Arts in early modern European history in 1969. From 1969 to 1971 he served as a secondary teacher of English and central African history in Mombasa Baptist High School in Mombasa, Kenya. He was also the school librarian. In 1971 he received an assistantship in the Graduate School of Library Science at the University of Illinois, where he earned his Master of Science in 1973. He was elected to four scholastic honor societies: Phi Alpha Theta (history), Beta Beta Beta (biology), Phi Kappa Phi (university-wide), and Beta Phi Mu (library and information science). He received the Phi Alpha Theta Scholarship Key in 1967. He joined the staff of the Dallas Public Library in the local history and genealogy division in 1973.

Mr. Bockstruck continued his studies at the Institute of Genealogy and Historical Research at Samford University, where he earned a certificate in 1973. He joined the faculty in 1974. He was the first recipient of its outstanding alumni award. He began teaching genealogical research methodology at Southern Methodist University in the School of Continuing Education from 1973, until he resigned to become a columnist with *The Dallas Morning News* in 1991. From 1994 to 2005, he was on the faculty of the Genealogical Institute of Mid-America at the University of Illinois Springfield. His biography was first listed in 1996 in *Who's Who in America*.

He was given the Award of Merit in 1982 by the National Genealogical Society and was named a Fellow in 1992. He was also named a Fellow of the Texas State Genealogical Society in 2008.

Active in America's hereditary societies, he was awarded honorary membership in the

107

Advisory Council of the Hereditary Society Community in the United States of America in 2004. He served on the Genealogy Committee of the American Library Association from 1974 to 1977 and was the first winner of the P. William Filby Prize for Genealogical Librarianship in 1999. The Northeast Texas Library System gave him its Lifetime Achievement Award in 2003. The Friends of the Dallas Public Library gave him the Lillian M. Bradshaw Award in 2008.

Publications by Lloyd deWitt Bockstruck:

1985 *Virginia's Colonial Soldiers*

1992 *Research in Texas*

1996 *Revolutionary War Bounty Land Grants Awarded by State Governments*

1998 *"Family Tree" Weekly Newspaper Columns from The Dallas Morning News 1991-1996*

2002 *Naval Pensioners of the United States, 1800-1850*

2005 *Denization and Naturalization in the British Colonies in America, 1607-1775*

2007 *Bounty and Donation Land Grants in British Colonial America*

2011 *Revolutionary War Pensions Awarded by State Governments 1775-1905, the General and Federal Governments prior to 1814 and by Private Acts of Congress to 1905*

2013 *The Name Is the Game: Onomatology and the Genealogist.*

Lloyd's ancestors were from Arkansas, Bermuda, Connecticut, Georgia, Illinois, Indiana, Kentucky, Louisiana, Maine, Maryland, Massachusetts, Missouri, New Hampshire, New Jersey, North Carolina, Pennsylvania, Rhode Island, South Carolina, Tennessee, Texas, Virginia, and West Virginia. His old world ancestors were from England, Germany, Ireland. Scotland, and Wales.

CPSIA information can be obtained
at www.ICGtesting.com
Printed in the USA
BVHW08s1740160818
524532BV00019B/294/P

9 780806 358314